Cybersecurity for Industrial Control Systems

SCADA, DCS, PLC, HMI, and SIS

Cybersecurity for Industrial Control Systems

SCADA, DCS, PLC, HMI, and SIS

Tyson Macaulay and Bryan Singer

CRC Press
Taylor & Francis Group
Boca Raton   London   New York

CRC Press is an imprint of the
Taylor & Francis Group, an **Informa** business

AN AUERBACH BOOK

CRC Press
Taylor & Francis Group
6000 Broken Sound Parkway NW, Suite 300
Boca Raton, FL 33487-2742

© 2012 by Taylor & Francis Group, LLC
CRC Press is an imprint of Taylor & Francis Group, an Informa business

No claim to original U.S. Government works

International Standard Book Number: 978-1-4398-0196-3 (Hardback)

Library of Congress Cataloging-in-Publication Data

Macaulay, Tyson.
    Cybersecurity for Industrial Control Systems : SCADA, DCS, PLC, HMI, and SIS / Tyson Macaulay, Bryan Singer.
        p. cm.
    Includes bibliographical references and index.
    ISBN 978-1-4398-0196-3 (hardcover : alk. paper)
    1. Process control--Security measures. 2. Automatic machinery--Security measures. 3. Computer security. I. Singer, Bryan. II. Title.

TS156.8.M328 2012
658.4'78--dc23   2011036559

Visit the Taylor & Francis Web site at
http://www.taylorandfrancis.com

and the CRC Press Web site at
http://www.crcpress.com

Contents

AUTHORS   ix

CHAPTER 1   INTRODUCTION   1
            Where This Book Starts and Stops   2
            Our Audience   3
            What Is an Industrial Control System?   6
            Is Industrial Control System Security Different Than
            Regular IT Security?   8
            Where Are ICS Used?   9
            ICS Compared to Safety Instrumented Systems   14
            What Has Changed in ICS That Raises New Concerns?   15
            Naming, Functionality, and Components of Typical ICS/
            SCADA Systems   18
                Supervisory Control and Data Acquisition (SCADA)   19
                Remote Terminal Unit (RTU)   20
                Distributed Control System (DCS)   20
                Programmable Logic Controllers (PLCs)   20
                Human–Machine Interface (HMI)   21
            Analogue versus IP Industrial Automation   22
            Convergence 101: It Is Not Just Process Data Crowding
            onto IP   25
            Convergence by Another Name   27
            Taxonomy of Convergence   28
                Triple-Play Convergence   29
                Transparent Convergence   30
                Blue-Sky Convergence   31
            The Business Drivers of IP Convergence   33

VI CONTENTS

Cost Drivers   33
Competitive Drivers   36
Regulatory Drivers   37
The Conflicting Priorities of Convergence   38
ICS Security Architecture and Convergence   40
The Discussions to Follow in This Book   43
Endnotes   44

CHAPTER 2   THREATS TO ICS   45
Threats to ICS: How Security Requirements Are Different
from ICS to IT   46
   Threat Treatment in ICS and IT   53
Threats to ICS   54
Threat-To and Threat-From   57
The Most Serious Threat to ICS   59
   Collateral Damage   60
      Whatever Happened to the Old-Fashioned E-Mail
      Virus?   60
   Money, Money, Money   62
   The Fatally Curious, Naïve, and Gullible   62
Hi-Jacking Malware   64
No Room for Amateurs   68
Taxonomy of Hi-Jacking Malware and Botnets   68
   Hi-Jacking Malware 101   69
      Characteristics of a Bot (Zombie/Drone)   69
The Reproductive Cycle of Modern Malware   72
A Socks 4/Sock 5/HTTP Connect Proxy   76
SMTP Spam Engines   78
Porn Dialers   78
Conclusions on ICS Threats   79
Endnotes   80

CHAPTER 3   ICS VULNERABILITIES   81
ICS Vulnerability versus IT Vulnerabilities   82
Availability, Integrity, and Confidentiality   83
Purdue Enterprise Reference Architecture   89
   PERA Levels   89
      Levels 5 and 4: Enterprise Systems   89
      Level 3: Operations Management   90
      Level 2: Supervisory Control   90
      Level 1: Local or Basic Control   91
      Level 0: Process   91
   An Ironic Comment on PERA   92
Data at Rest, Data in Use, Data in Motion   93
Distinguishing Business, Operational, and Technical
Features of ICS   95

ICS Vulnerabilities   98
    Management Vulnerabilities   99
    Operational Vulnerabilities   100
    Technical Vulnerabilities   105
Functional Vulnerabilities   106
ICS Technical Vulnerability Class Breakdown   111
    Technical Vectors of Attack   113
IT Devices on the ICS Network   114
Interdependency with IT   115
Green Network Stacks   116
Protocol Inertia   116
Limited Processing Power and Memory Size   118
Storms/DOS of Various Forms   119
Fuzzing   120
MITM and Packet Injection   121
Summary   123
Endnotes   123

CHAPTER 4   RISK ASSESSMENT TECHNIQUES   125
Introduction   125
Contemporary ICS Security Analysis Techniques   126
    North American Electricity Reliability Council (NERC)   126
    National Institute of Standards and Technology (NIST)   128
    Department of Homeland Security (DHS) ICS Risk
    Assessment Processes   129
INL National SCADA Test Bed Program (NSTB): Control
System Security Assessment   130
INL Vulnerability Assessment Methodology   131
INL Metrics-Based Reporting for Risk Assessment   133
Ideal-Based Risk Assessment and Metrics   134
CCSP Cyber Security Evaluation Tool (CSET)   135
    U.S. Department of Energy: Electricity Sector Cyber
    Security Risk Management Process Guideline   136
Evolving Risk Assessment Processes   137
    Consequence Matrices   138
    Safety Integrity Levels and Security Assurance Levels   140
Security Assurance Level   141
SAL-Based Assessments   144
SAL Workflow   145
Future of SAL   147
    Overall Equipment Effectiveness (Assessment)   148
Security OEE   149
Putting OEE Metrics Together   152
    Network-Centric Assessment   153
Network-Centric Compromise Indicators   155
    Assessing Threat Agents, Force, and Velocity   155

Other Network Infrastructure That Can Be Used for
Network-Centric Analysis and ICS Security   157
Network-Centric Assessment Caveats   159
Conclusion   160
Endnotes   161

CHAPTER 5   WHAT IS NEXT IN ICS SECURITY?   163
The Internet of Things   163
IPv6   164
 There Is a New Internet Protocol in Town   164
 In Brief: What Is IPv6?   164
 What Does IPv6 Mean for My Business in General?   165
 What Does the Switch to IPv6 Mean for the Security of
 My ICS Network?   166
 What Will the Move to IPv6 Require, for IT and ICS?   167
ICS v6 Test Lab Designs   168
 Stage 1 Test Environment: Introduce IPv6   169
 Stage 2 Test Environment: Sense IPv6   170
 Stage 3 Test Environment: Dual-Stack Testing   170
 Stage 4 Test Environment   171
 Stage 5 Test Environment   172
 Dual Stacking   174
 ICS and Cellular Wireless   176
 Private Architecture and Cellular Wireless   176
 v6 Security Testing Methodology for ICS Devices   180
IPv6 and ICS Sensors   182
 Pros and Cons of IPv6 and Low-Power (Wireless) Devices   183
A Few Years Yet...   185
Endnotes   185

INDEX   187

Authors

Tyson Macaulay is the security liaison officer (SLO) for Bell Canada. In this role, he is responsible for technical and operational risk management solutions for Bell's largest enterprise clients.

Macaulay leads security initiatives addressing large, complex, technology solutions including physical and logical (IT) assets, and regulatory/legal compliance requirements. He supports engagements involving multinational companies and international governments. Macaulay also supports the development of engineering and security standards through the Professional Engineers of Ontario and the International Standards Organization (ISO) SC 27 Committee.

Macaulay's leadership encompasses a broad range of industry sectors from the defense industry to high-tech start-ups. His expertise includes operational risk management programs, technical services, and incident management processes. He has successfully served as prime architect for large-scale security implementations in both public and private sector institutions, working on projects from conception through development to implementation. Macaulay is a respected thought leader with publications dating from 1993. His work has covered authorship of peer-reviewed white papers, IT security governance programs, technical and integration services, and incident management processes. Further information on Macaulay's publications and practice areas can be found online at: www.tysonmacaulay.com.

Previously, Macaulay served as director of risk management for a U.S. defense contractor in Ottawa, Electronic Warfare Associates (EWA; 2001–2005), and founded General Network Services (GNS; 1996–2001). Macaulay's career began as a research consultant for the Federal Department of Communications (DoC) on information networks, where he helped develop the first generation of Internet services for the DoC in the 1990s.

Bryan L. Singer, CISM, CISSP, CAP, is principal consultant for Kenexis Consulting Corporation. Singer has more than 15 years experience in information technology security, including 7 years specializing in industrial automation and control systems security, critical infrastructure protection, and counterterrorism. His background focuses on software development, network design, information security, and industrial security. Industry experience includes health care, telecommunications, water/wastewater, automotive, food and beverage, pharmaceuticals, fossil and hydropower generation, oil and gas, and several others. He has specialized in process intelligence and manufacturing disciplines such as historians, industrial networking, power and energy management (PEMS), manufacturing enterprise systems (MES), laboratory information management systems (LIMS), enterprise resource planning (ERP), condition-based monitoring (CBM), and others.

Singer began his professional career with the U.S. Army as an intelligence analyst. After the military, he worked in various critical infrastructure fields in software development and systems design, including security. Singer has worked for great companies such as EnteGreat, Rockwell Automation, FluidIQs, and Wurldtech before joining Kenexis Consulting and cofounding Kenexis Security in 2008. At Kenexis, he is responsible for development, deployment, and management of industrial network design and security services from both a safety and a system architecture perspective.

Singer is also the cochairman of ISA-99 Security Standard, a former board member of the Department of Homeland Security's Process Control Systems Forum, member of Idaho National Labs recommended practices commission, U.S. technical expert to IEC, North American Electronics Reliability Corporation (NERC) drafting team member for NERC CIP, and other industry roles.

1

INTRODUCTION

This book is either ambitious, brave, or reckless approaching a topic as rapidly evolving as industrial control system (ICS) security. From the advent of ICS-targeted malicious software such as Stuxnet to the advanced persistent threats posed by organized crime and state-sponsored entities, ICS is in the crosshairs and practices and controls considered safe today may be obsolete tomorrow. Possibly more so than in more traditional IT security, because of the differences inherent in ICS.

We are taking a chance by addressing highly technical topic—the security of industrial automation and process control, also known as ICS security—from both technical and management perspectives, and at times from a more philosophical perspective. The reason for this approach is that a substantial amount of ad hoc and anecdotal technical material and analysis already exist, and this material would benefit from a broader treatment that includes business-level topics such as business case development and compliance and, ultimately, more effective enterprise risk management.

On the face of it, securing communications and operations in industrial automation and process control offers unique challenges in that not only do we deal with the traditional data and communications security requirements found on any given IT network, but we also must deal with the reality of the physics of a process in which motion is controlled and manipulated through data-dependent systems and computers—physical changes that can impact a system in myriad ways. These include costly production stoppages, maintenance failures and repairs, and even hazardous releases and dangerous failures.

In some cases, the published standards and recognized and generally accepted approaches for ICS security and traditional IT security can appear so similar as to be superfluous; however, they are developed to serve substantially different objectives. It is these few substantially different objectives that inspire this book, in which we intend to discuss ICS security requirements coupled with operational and management solutions.

The overall objective of this book is to improve industrial and enterprise risk management in this age of Internet protocol (IP) convergence, recognizing that industrial systems require the balancing of many engineering and business requirements more tightly than is often the case in a data-centric IT system.

Where This Book Starts and Stops

The mark of a mature technical discipline is when discussion around operational details and nuances is balanced by discussion of management strategies and tactics: how to get the best results from the technology at the granular, device level, and how to coordinate and consolidate entire systems into an efficient whole. Evidence of a mature practice manifests when even the most complex technical and engineering subjects can be expressed in a meaningful way at any level of an organization so that risk impacts and mitigations can be clearly communicated at all levels.

Evidence of an immature discipline is readily apparent in inconsistent practices, dependence on "experts and qualitative measures" and a solid dose of faith in what the experts provide in order to gain a comfort factor of risk reduction to business operations.

The domain of ICS has been expanding rapidly with security solutions and solutions vendors relative to the evidence of threats specifically against process control assets. However, compared to the related field of IT security, there is still a relatively small amount of management-level guidance available for the operational managers developing business cases, risk managers performing assessments, or auditors seeking context against which to evaluate the adequacy and balance of controls and safeguards relative to risks. This book is intended in part to address the imbalance between technical details and information about ICS security and management-level guidance specific to process control security.

By management-level guidance we mean information that can be consumed by those trying to balance the business requirements of risk reduction, production, and operational budgets into an effective blended strategy: how much risk can you treat versus how much risk can you transfer versus risk you can accept. This balance between treatment, transfer, and acceptance is fundamental to overall risk management and does not require deep technical knowledge. Technical knowledge and information is an important input to this process, and as such we refer the reader to the many technical publications related to ICS security—from vendor white papers to National Institute of Standards and Technology (NIST) and International Organization for Standardization (ISO) standards.

This book is not about process control security architectures. Where it is useful to reference or provide security architectures we will do so, but we will reference prior work in this area such as that from NIST 800-53 revision 2, "Recommended Security Controls for Federal Information System," and 800-82, "Guide to Industrial Control System (ICS) Security," ISA-99 Industrial Automation and Control Systems Security Standard, and the UK National Security Advice Centre.[1]

This book is not an attempt to catalog known vulnerabilities or specific attacks and malware, such as Stuxnet, associated with process control systems. Such an attempt would be futile because such a list would be obsolete long before this book got off the editor's desk and into print. For information about some of the latest process control vulnerabilities, the reader is directed to sources such as the Computer Emergency Response Team[2] or the Process Control System Forum.[3] While these subjects are referenced, there are plenty of resources available that will discuss technical vulnerabilities. Rather, this text deals with the processes and disciplines required to proactively seek, understand, and address such vulnerabilities, and also with looking at the industrial processes in a new way: understanding how unintentional and intentional actions can result in systemic faults and failures that could impact safe and reliable operations in today's modern industrial processes. It is in these areas of failure analysis that we often find opportunities for failures on a day-to-day basis that go largely unnoticed. Until something anomalous occurs. Understanding these possible failure modes and process hazards is the first step in designing a more robust system that resists faults and helps ensure continued operation of mission-critical systems.

Our Audience

We intend to satisfy a wide range of readers in this book; this is where we become most ambitious.

For the IT or ICS security novice there will be plenty of useful background data about the world of ICS and, more importantly, context. Context about the various forms of process control, how they relate to each other, and how they relate to IT systems that might be covered by the same job description, if not residing on the same networks!

For the people dealing with ICS and security on a day-in day-out basis, this book will provide a broad framework for understanding and addressing both technical and business requirements. This book will provide some granular detail but is not intended as a how-to model for hardening process control systems in a step-by-step manner. It will, however, provide many useful insights and guidance on how to assess and manage threats and risks facing ICS, and how to communicate the business case rationale to obtain the resources to address these threats and risks. The material covered in this book is not specific to any particular industry or ICS; it has been specifically authored to help practitioners from any industrial sector, whether they are supporting a legacy system with proprietary protocols and networks migrating to IP, or the latest IPv6 technologies (see Chapter 5 for more on this topic specifically).

The rise of Ethernet usage on the shop floor and the continued need for information visibility throughout the entire enterprise drive ever-increasing convergence between the IT networks and ICS networks. For the experienced IT security guru, this book will provide a good introduction to "the other IT": industrial control systems, often known by related terms such as supervisory control and data acquisition (SCADA) and distributed control systems (DCS), to name a couple.

This soup of acronyms can create a confusing picture and barriers to understanding. ICS, SCADA, DCS, and so forth, are ubiquitous terms that must be understood by IT types. Each term has a different implication for technical architecture, usage, and potential threats, risks, and hazards.

Previously, these industrial environments were disconnected and "closed" due to communications incompatibility with Ethernet and other common local area network (LAN) protocols and the ICS protocols such as Modbus, Profibus, ControlNet, DeviceNet, and more. Today, these protocols are often entirely converged with IT systems on Ethernet and IP networks combining the infrastructures and allowing seamless integration across various layer 1 physical media types (copper, fiber, wireless) and communications protocols.

For auditors of IT systems, this book will be a source of baseline data about controls and safeguards that might be found in the ICS environments as they migrate from analogue to digital and especially IP-based networks.

Forensics practitioners and accident investigators may find utility in this book due to the observations and recommendations made related to safety systems versus ICS, and the manner in which threats and risks might be assessed and ultimately prioritized. We would not presume to indicate any fault or blame associated with threat and risk management methodologies different from those in this book; however, the information, methodologies, controls, and safeguards mentioned in this book should be at least partially represented in most comprehensive ICS security practices.

ICS engineers may find valuable information about how to relate IT security issues to a more familiar view of generally accepted ICS best practices and disciplines such as process safety, efficiency, quality management, and performance management. This book will also assist ICS engineers in the determination of process hazards, mitigation of safety risks, and implementation of engineered safeguards to avoid dangerous failures or impacts to production and supply chain operations.

In places like the United States, regulators and legislators have shown forbearance when it comes to setting standards for process controls, even around the most sensitive infrastructures. For instance, the Federal Energy Regulatory Commission (FERC)[4] allows the industry-lead North American Electricity Reliability Council (NERC)[5] to establish security standards for the industry, even though the standards were essentially first approved by FERC before being deemed mandatory for NERC members. NERC is actually a North American organization, including energy suppliers in Canada; so the U.S. FERC has pretty much legislated for other countries at the same time. Other jurisdictions like the European Union appear to be headed in a similar direction. At the time of the writing of this book, considerable additional regulatory and legislative efforts are moving forward, including recommended practices and requirements from the Nuclear Regulatory Commission[6] and the Chemical Facility Anti-Terrorism Standards defined in 6 CFR 27, Appendix A.[7] These and similar efforts continue to develop throughout the world's governments as the need to protect critical infrastructure becomes increasingly clear. This book aspires to contribute to those discussions about ICS security.

What Is an Industrial Control System?

Process control system (PCS), distributed control system (DCS), and supervisory control and data acquisition (SCADA) are names frequently applied to the systems that control, monitor, and manage large production systems. The systems are often in critical infrastructures industries, such as electric power generators, transportation systems, dams, chemical facilities, petrochemical operations, pipelines, and others, giving the security of PCS, DCS, and SCADA systems evaluated importance in the increasingly networked world we live in.

SCADA especially is a term that has fairly recently been deprecated. In 2002 the International Society of Automation (ISA) started work on security standards for what it called industrial automation and control systems (IACS), under the aegis of its 99 standard.

IACS included SCADA services and reflected the wider and broader industrial infrastructures that were based on IP and interfaced with IT systems. IACS was further shortened in 2006 when the Department of Homeland Security (DHS) published *Mitigations for Vulnerabilities Found in Control System (CS) Networks*. Finally, in 2008, the National Institute of Standards and Technology applied the current compromise name, industry control systems (ICS), in its landmark publication of NIST 800-82: *Guide to Industrial Control System Security*.

In this chapter we will distinguish between PCS, DCS, and SCADA systems as a matter of formal detail, but for the most part we intend all three systems when using the term *industrial control systems* (ICS): as a preliminary summary, ICS gathers information from a variety of endpoint devices about the current status of a production process, which may be fully or partially automated. Historians, typical IT systems within process control environments, gather information concerning the production process. PCS, DCS, SCADA, and so forth, read values and interact based upon automated logic alarms and events requiring operators interaction, or report automated system state changes.

A process control system allows operators to make control decisions, which might then be relayed upstream, downstream, or to parallel processes for execution by the same system. These systems could be within the four walls of one building, or could be spread throughout a potentially massive geographical region (in the case for items such as pipelines, power distribution, water and wastewater management.) For example, an ICS might gather information from endpoint devices that allow operators to assess that a leak may have opened in a pipeline. The system aggregates this information at a central site, which (hopefully) contains intelligence and analytics alerting a control station and operators that the leak has occurred. Operators then carry out necessary analysis to determine if and how the leak may impact operations, safety, and regulations (environmental, health, and safety).

ICS displays the information gathered from endpoint devices in a logical and organized fashion, and keeps a history of the parameters received from the endpoint device. If the leak under investigation required that pressure in the pipeline be reduced or even that the pipeline be shut down, then these operational instructions may be issued from the control station through the ICS. Another possibility is that the ICS is intended for monitoring but not active intervention, in which case the operators would dispatch maintenance teams according to the coordinates provided by the process control system.

This example starts to reveal the fact that control systems can be relatively simple or incredibly complex. More often than not, the systems are more complex than is readily apparent on the surface, which in part distinguishes them from IT systems. For instance, where the traditional IT space deals with a fairly limited set of operating systems, communications protocols, and Open System Interconnection (OSI) model layer 1 (physical) and layer 2 (data link) device vendors (as illustrated in Figure 1.3), a typical process environment can represent hundreds of devices from different vendors with different specifications, protocols, and physical deployment requirements.

Systems may be solely intended for the purpose of collecting, displaying, and archiving information from endpoint devices. For instance, urban traffic flow information from various intersections around a large city is used for both day-to-day governance and long-term urban planning. Alternately, ICS in a nuclear power plant or a municipal water system may have the ability to apply either automatic, semiautomatic, or operator-controlled changes. It is important to note at this point that ICS are not necessarily the same as safety systems, and in some cases are completely distinct. More on the difference between ICS and safety systems will follow in this section.

Is Industrial Control System Security Different Than Regular IT Security?

Comparing techniques, tools, and terminology, ICS security is not entirely different from current IT security. There are differences, however. These differences largely center around the following principles:

- Almost all ICS security failures have physical consequences, impacts that are frequently more severe and immediate.
- ICS security issues often manifest initially as traditional maintenance failures or other nuisance trips and process stoppages, making them difficult to diagnose and remedy. Anomalies are more prevelant.
- ICS security can be more difficult to manage: old systems that can't be patched or upgraded, no luxury of development and test environments, massively dispersed assets with mandatory requirements for frequent remote access, and conventional protections such as antivirus or firewall that may not be able to be utilized.
- Cyber threats to an ICS include myriad additional threat vectors, including nontypical network protocols, commands that cannot be blocked due to safety or production issues (alarm and event traffic, for example), and otherwise valid communications used by an attacker in invalid ways.

What is more, most legacy and even many contemporary ICS assets were not planned and budgeted with IT-like security as part of cost of goods calculations; therefore the business margins simply do not support additional security, especially in regulated industries where tariffs are approved by regulators. Many of these industries are already heavily regulated, and operators are naturally reluctant to add any additional complexity into a process if it complicates compliance.

Given that convergence between IT and ICS networks is a relatively new discipline, ICS security as a domain has much it may productively learn from the far more mature, larger IT security domain.

Threat and risk assessment and management are far more developed as are the language and tools for addressing threats and risks is a systemic fashion using standardized terminology. Conversely, off-the-shelf IT security controls and safeguards are not ready to be applied wholesale to ICS: there needs to be a reconciliation and understanding of the potential for kinetic impact and lasting physical damage to product quality, operations assets, and potentially irrecoverable downstream and upstream impacts to customers, partners, and suppliers.

Last, because of overlapping but not necessarily apparent impacts shared between IT and ICS, people may be reluctant to take action. For instance, if an industry has explicit safety regulations to apply and has built to these mandatory safety standards, then security may not even be on the table! It can take a lot in some cases to convince someone that a security issue is not addressed by a safety design that has been accepted by a regulator.

Where Are ICS Used?

ICS are used throughout modern economic ecosystems, in factories, energy systems, bakeries, automotive manufacturers, breweries, pharmaceutical manufacturers, hospitals, entertainment parks, and even in ubiquitous building automation for heating, ventilation and air conditioning (HVAC) systems, elevators, and other modern conveniences. However, not all information assets within these industries are ICS, they too are full of IT systems: that being said, the interfaces between ICS and IT are so multiple and manifest that ICS and IT almost always interface and affect each other within a given plant/business and industry. IT systems focus on the management, movement, and manipulation of data; ICS focuses on the management, movement, and manipulation of physical system such as valves, actuators, drives, motors, and the production of the associated products.

A useful perspective for understanding the operational domain and prevalence of ICS versus IT systems might be a review of the critical infrastructure sectors as defined by Homeland Security Presidential Directive 7 (HSPD-7) from 2003.[8] HSPD-7 defined 17 sectors with different government agencies accountable for the protection of these sectors.[9] Table 1.1 outlines these sectors and identifies how they frequently represent a major operational domain for ICS assets.

Table 1.1 Critical Infrastructure Sectors under HSPD 7

SECTOR	ACCOUNTABLE AGENCY	DESCRIPTION	USE OF INDUSTRIAL PROCESS CONTROL SYSTEMS VERSUS IT SYSTEMS
Agriculture and food	Departments of Agriculture, and Health and Human Services, Food and Drug Administration	Provides for the fundamental need for food. The infrastructure includes supply chains for feed and crop production. Carries out the postharvesting of the food supply, including processing and retail sales.	Large use of process control systems, especially in food processing.
Defense and industrial base	Department of Defense	Supplies the military with the means to protect the nation by producing weapons, aircraft, and ships and providing essential services, including information technology and supply and maintenance.	Some heavy industry would be included in this sector, indicating the presence of process control.
Energy	Department of Energy	Provides the electric power used by all sectors and the refining, storage, and distribution of oil and gas. The sector is divided into electricity and oil and natural gas.	Large user of process control systems.
Public health and health care	Department of Health and Human Services	Mitigates the risk of disasters and attacks and also provides recovery assistance if an attack occurs. The sector consists of health departments, clinics, and hospitals.	Moderate to small user or process control—most systems would be IT systems managing information.
National monuments and icons	Department of the Interior	Memorializes or represents monuments, physical structures, objects, or geographical sites that are widely recognized to represent the nation's heritage, traditions, or values, or widely recognized to represent important national cultural, religious, historical, or political significance.	Moderate to small user or process control—most systems would be IT systems managing information.

Banking and finance	Department of the Treasury	Provides the financial infrastructure of the nation. This sector consists of commercial banks, insurance companies, mutual funds, government-sponsored enterprises, pension funds, and other financial institutions that carry out transactions.	Most systems are entirely IT in origin and use. Little to no process control systems.
Drinking water and water treatment systems	Environmental Protection Agency	Provides sources of safe drinking water from more than 53,000 community water systems and properly treated wastewater from more than 16,000 publicly owned treatment works.	Large user of process control systems.
Chemical	DHS—Office of Infrastructure Protection	Transforms natural raw materials into commonly used products benefiting society's health, safety, and productivity. The chemical sector produces more than 70,000 products that are essential to automobiles, pharmaceuticals, food supply, electronics, water treatment, health, construction, and other necessities.	Large user of process control systems.
Commercial facilities	DHS—Office of Infrastructure Protection	Includes prominent commercial centers, office buildings, sports stadiums, theme parks, and other sites where large numbers of people congregate to pursue business activities, conduct personal commercial transactions, or enjoy recreational pastimes.	Large user of process control systems.
Dams	DHS—Office of Infrastructure Protection	Manages water retention structures, including levees, more than 77,000 conventional dams, navigation locks, canals (excluding channels), and similar structures, including larger and nationally symbolic dams that are major components of other critical infrastructures that provide electricity and water.	Large user of process control systems.

(Continued)

Table 1.1 Critical Infrastructure Sectors under HSPD 7 (Continued)

SECTOR	ACCOUNTABLE AGENCY	DESCRIPTION	USE OF INDUSTRIAL PROCESS CONTROL SYSTEMS VERSUS IT SYSTEMS
Emergency services	DHS—Office of Infrastructure Protection	Saves lives and property from accidents and disaster. This sector includes fire, rescue, emergency medical services, and law enforcement organizations.	Most systems are entirely IT in origin and use. Little to no process control systems.
Nuclear reactors, materials, and waste	DHS—Office of Infrastructure Protection	Provides nuclear power, which accounts for approximately 20% of the nation's electrical generating capacity. The sector includes commercial nuclear reactors and nonpower nuclear reactors used for research, testing, and training; nuclear materials used in medical, industrial, and academic settings; nuclear fuel fabrication facilities; the decommissioning of reactors; and the transportation, storage, and disposal of nuclear materials and waste.	Large user of process control systems.
Information technology	DHS—Office of Cyber Security and Communications	Produces information technology and includes hardware manufacturers, software developers, and service providers, as well as the Internet as a key resource.	Most systems are entirely IT in origin and use. While large infrastructures are remotely managed in this sector, the devices are orthodox Ethernet/IP devices. Some process control systems may be present in manufacturers.
Communications	DHS—Office of Cyber Security and Communications	Provides wired, wireless, and satellite communications to meet the needs of businesses and governments.	Most systems are entirely IT in origin and use. While large infrastructures are remotely managed in this sector, the devices are orthodox Ethernet/IP devices.

Postal and shipping	Transportation Security Administration	Delivers private and commercial letters, packages, and bulk assets. The U.S. Postal Service and other carriers provide the services of this sector.	Large user of process control systems.
Transportation systems	Transportation Security Administration and U.S. Coast Guard	Enables movement of people and assets that are vital to our economy, mobility, and security with the use of aviation, ships, rail, pipelines, highways, trucks, buses, and mass transit.	Large user of process control systems.
Government facilities	Immigration and Customs Enforcement, Federal Protective Service	Ensures continuity of functions for facilities owned and leased by the government, including all federal, state, territorial, local, and tribal government facilities located in the United States and abroad.	Most systems are entirely IT in origin and use. Some process control systems may be present for management of large facilities.

ICS Compared to Safety Instrumented Systems

ICS includes safety instrumented systems (SIS), which are specifically hardened ICS elements built for high reliability and associated with failing safe. SIS have functional elements contributing substantially to operational safety and risk management, and often share technical architectures and features with more general purpose ICS. Understanding the purposes and function of SIS is critical to managing the security of ICS. The distinction of ICS versus SIS is worth making because the design and deployment of safety systems, like IT systems, is often related to but different from ICS.

SIS are generally designed with a single purpose in mind: avoiding dangerous situations in the production system by stopping or shutting down processes if unsafe conditions develop. SIS are for monitoring the state of the ICS infrastructure; they are not designed for managing production processes, they are dedicated to process safety. Additionally, SIS are typically implemented as compensating controls for known or anticipated hardware failure rates. These failure rates are established through recognized and generally accepted good engineering practices adopted by both asset owners and vendors, driven by industry standards such as ISA-84, IEC 61508, IEC 61511, and others.

These controls help prevent dangerous failure conditions from occurring as a result of hardware failure in a moving process. These random but probabilistic (can be predicted as a likelihood over a given time—just not "when" within that time) events are less considered in ICS security, which focuses more on the potential vectors that could allow dangerous conditions to arise through unintended consequences of user actions, directed threats, or systematic faults and failures that arise through issues such as network failure, application faults, or inability to see or properly respond to system and process messages.

Safety and protection systems often have additional safety requirements that may not be consistent or relevant to cyber security requirements. These systems include the safety systems in use in upstream production; for instance, chemical and petrochemical plants as identified in ANSI/ISA-84, IEC 61508 and 61511, and API-14C; and protective functions as identified in IEEE Power Engineering Society Standards.

This notion of controls and safeguards from probabilistic threats inherent in SIS will be revisited later in this book, during the discussion of security integrity levels (SILs) versus security assurance levels (SALs).

An important note considering SIS is that it is a common fallacy to assume that the ICS does not require additional security protection because of the SIS. There are several points that, once understood, dispel this impression of SIS supporting all required ICS security:

1. SIS and safety, as a discipline, primarily address one key aspect of anomalous process behavior: protection against entropic (random) hardware faults of an unintentional nature.

2. SIS often use the same technology platform as other ICS, meaning that ICS vulnerabilities may well be common mode failures to SIS, allowing an attacker to compromise both control and safety logic in disrupting a process at once or using the same tradecraft. For instance, an existing issue is that engineering workstations (EWSs) are used to configure both process control devices and safety systems, which means that a threat agent could compromise the ICS and the SIS by gaining access to the EWS. This issue is amplified by the prevalence of the Windows operating system on EWSs.

3. In order for the SIS to function properly, it must be connected in some way to the ICS to monitor electronic function and determine if safety logic must be invoked. As such, there really is no such thing as a disconnected safety system. Knowledgeable attackers could bypass or suspend safety logic in conducting an attack.

4. Just as in other ICS, there is an increasing trend in integrating SIS on IP-based networks, including convergence with traditional business systems and evolving enterprise resource planning (ERP) systems.

There are currently a number of private and closed source studies being conducted on the security of SIS, and it is likely that more information will be available publicly in the coming months and years.

What Has Changed in ICS That Raises New Concerns?

ICS technology has been evolving since the earliest systems for remote monitoring and controlling of industrial processes were put in place in the 1960s. Prior to this period, manual operator observations and intervention were the norm, aided by networks of pipes with gauges that allowed very simple forms of process monitoring. (Think of the steam pressure gauge on a boiler, which might be available on the bridge of a ship.) The advent of transistors and modern electronics made the process control systems as we know them today possible, allowing industrial processes to be made both more efficient and more pervasive. Of course, ICS also improved the ability to detect and respond to dangerous situations, and thereby mitigate some of the risks associated with massively scaling up industrial production processes in order to gain economies of scale. As we will discuss soon, while ICSs are not safety systems, they allow processes to be managed with a significantly greater degree of assurance that could be attained by applying pre-ICS techniques, such as manual observations by larger staffs of industrial workers.

As might be expected with any new technology, in the earlier days of ICS there were many different suppliers, each with a proprietary technology. Standards for process control communication did not exist at the birth of the process control market, so each vendor tended to develop the necessary technology to connect remote endpoint devices to the networks and transport the data to central data historians and management consoles. Gradually, the ICS market consolidated through attrition, mergers, and acquisitions to the point we are at today, with perhaps half a dozen dominant process control vendors from an original field of probably hundreds. In addition to market consolidation, a wide variety of new requirements have emerged for process control systems relative to their initial foundations. For instance, the period in which ICS has been evolving has paralleled the evolution of business information systems, which moved from carbon paper and dictation to e-mail and Internet commerce during the same period. Similarly, a host of new regulatory requirements, from financial reporting to environmental monitoring, have come into effect while process control systems evolved. These factors mean that process control systems had an increasing need to interface with other information and reporting systems in the business.

Recent industrial history has demonstrated that the life cycle of a control system is now between 15 and 30 years. As little as even 15 years ago, network and software security was not a top priority in the control systems environment, and ICS networks were not using the same underlying protocols as the other business networks within organizations. (Recall that 15 years ago technologies such as Novell and Banyan dominated the LAN market, while IEEE 802.3 Ethernet was just evolving. Internet protocol was available, but typically only as a fiddly third-party software extension.) The IT and ICS networks were conventionally and technically isolated. Control systems were stand-alone assets not connected to business networks or the outside world except perhaps for very slow modems that would be used for remote management and maintenance. Competition among process control vendors and a drive for simpler to manage networks and cost savings have driven ICS from highly proprietary, custom-built, stand-alone systems to those that use commercial off-the-shelf (COTS) hardware and software components. With the convergence of ICS onto the same IP and operating system platforms as other generic business tools and applications comes increased risk.

In the last 6 months of 2010, Symantec stated in its Internet security threat report[10] that it "recorded more vulnerabilities in 2010 than in any previous year since starting this report. Furthermore, the new vendors affected by a vulnerability rose to 1,914, a 161% increase over the prior year."

The Symantec evidence makes it plain that malicious code and cyber threats continue to grow as the Internet expands and penetrates further and further into both business and personal applications, but how does this translate to threat levels related to ICS assets?

Some analysts estimated that 10% of all IP-enabled devices in existence today are ICS devices.[11] This number of connected devices (versus people via PC and laptops) is expected to grow dramatically with a compound growth rate of 30% from 2012 to 2020—reaching as much 7 billion devices by that time and completely outnumbering people-oriented connections.[12] Much of this connectivity will be through wireless cellular technology, but also through more traditional Ethernet LANs; but all of it will be IP-based and especially IPv6 (see the last chapter for a discussion of IPv6). Connected devices are all around us, yet their profiles and exposure to IP-based threats are hardly known relative to the discussion and effort associated with IT controls and safeguards. Granted, any IT controls and safeguards can be directly applied to ICS, but the way they are applied is always based on a risk calculation, and ICS risks are distinct from IT risks, as discussed previously.

More encouraging is that awareness of ICS security has risen dramatically in the last few years. The U.S. Department of Homeland Security recognizes the importance of ICS security education and awareness and offers funding for industrial control security research and tools for managing and even procuring secure process control systems. For instance, DHS has published the cyber security procurement language document as a means to help asset owners integrate security into their control system's security life cycle. There is also the Idaho National Labs Recommended Practices Commission, and the Control Systems Security Program (CSSP) at the U.S. Computer Emergency Readiness Team (US-CERT[13]).

Naming, Functionality, and Components of Typical ICS/SCADA Systems

Process control system (PCS), distributed control system (DCS), and supervisory control and data acquisition (SCADA) are names frequently applied to the systems that control, monitor, and management of large production systems. The systems are often in critical infrastructures industries such as electric power generators, transportation systems, dams, chemical facilities, petrochemical operations, telecommunication systems, pipelines, and others, giving the security of PCS, DCS, and SCADA systems elevated importance in the increasingly networked world we live in.

This section distinguishes between PCS, DCS, and SCADA systems as a matter of formal detail, but the commonly used *ICS* term continues to be applied to each system type. The most significant difference is in the local cultural usage of the terms related to the process. The underlying technical components and exposure to cybersecurity threats are common across all. As a preliminary summary, all ICS gathers information from a variety of endpoint devices about the current status of a production process, which may be fully or partially automated. Historians, typical IT systems within process control environments, gather information and perform basic or complex computational analysis of process variables to produce key performance indicators (KPIs) to demonstrate actual points in time statistics or trending of production processes over time. PCS, DCS, SCADA, and so on, read values, interact based upon automated logic, issue alarms on events requiring operators' interaction, or report automated system state changes.

According to ISA Standard 99, the terms *industrial automation* and *process control system* include "control systems used in manufacturing and processing plants and facilities, building environmental control systems, geographically dispersed operations such as utilities (i.e., electricity, gas, and water), pipelines and petroleum production and distribution facilities, and other industries and applications such as transportation networks, that use automated or remotely controlled or monitored assets." Process control communications methods include a wide range of technologies, some of which are used by IT systems and some that are completely unique to the discipline: from pneumatic tubes and hydraulics to leased phone lines, dial-up phone lines, Ethernet (IEEE 802.3), cellular (analogue, PCS, 3G, 4G), satellite, and point-to-point microwave circuits.

In the following discussion we will review the various component parts of ICS, which are sometimes (confusingly) referred to as though they were interchangeable in function and concept with ICS.

Supervisory Control and Data Acquisition (SCADA)

SCADA refers to the centralized systems that control production infrastructures. *SCADA* is frequently used interchangeably with *process control* and *ICS*; however, the distinction may lie in the observation that SCADA systems are considered to support *coordination* of infrastructures rather than exercising control over the discrete element of these infrastructures. (See distributed control system [DCS] definition below.) ICS encompasses both coordination and control functions. A *SCADA system might be considered event driven*, where an event may be either scheduled or unscheduled, while a *DCS is process state driven*, where a state is comparable to an anticipated stage in a process and the activities that are required at a given stage. A DCS is primarily interested in process trends, a SCADA system in process events that are to be aggregated and reported by DCS. A SCADA system looks for unscheduled changes of state that simply cannot be missed.

Remote Terminal Unit (RTU)

In an ICS, RTUs collect data from the field devices and convert them from analogue to digital signals for transmission to a control center where they may be stored by a data historian or displayed to operators from terminals. RTUs may also receive control signals from the process control computer and relay them to the individual field sensors. RTUs convert and relay telemetry and data. RTUs are frequently the simplest of the process control devices with limited intelligence or processing; however, RTUs designed and built within the recent past are sometimes capable of more than data collection and relay. Added-value elements such as highly granular *time tagging down to 1 ms* is readily available and relieves some of the network-based risks associated with latency. In fact, many major RTUs come with some form of PLC-like functionality, such as higher-level processing, for instance, *autoreclose* and remote configuration.[14]

Distributed Control System (DCS)

A DCS refers to a system in which the controller elements are distributed rather than centralized (as in SCADA), with each component and discrete subsystem controlled by one or more controllers. DCSs consider the process variable's present and past states to be the main criteria driving the decisions and judgments. DCS software tasks are generally run sequentially and chronologically, rather than being event driven. DCS-based alarms or alerts are not generated when a point changes state, but when that particular process is run. Alarms and alerts are secondary in importance to the DCS process displays. While a DCS may seem unduly simple, the generation and display of data, especially analogue trends and standard process blocks, are important operational information that can be easily rendered into user-friendly displays and visualization, making interpretation and subsequent management easier for both operators and engineers.

Programmable Logic Controllers (PLCs)

PLCs may be used in place of, or in addition to, RTUs; a PLC is designed for real-time use in rugged environments and may contain logic and programming to control local functions that may not need to communicate with the centralized SCADA service, or be executed from the DCS. Connected to sensors and actuators, PLCs are categorized by the number and type of I/O ports they provide and by their I/O scan rate.[15]

PLCs will often be designed with the necessary logic to protect the assets under management in the event contact is lost with the main SCADA or DCS computer. Historically, PLCs were viewed as simple devices with very limited processing capability. Emerging trends among most suppliers today is to drop the term *PLC* in favor of the more general term of *controller*, with an emphasis on the deployed architecture of the system. This architecture may include the human–machine interfaces, convergence of multiple process types, and the ability to either receive and respond to process events or support more advanced process control features such as data aggregation, advanced reporting, or highly specialized production process methodologies such as fuzzy logic optimization.

Human–Machine Interface (HMI)

An HMI is the place where human operators go to manipulate the infrastructure through the ICS. An HMI an be can be touch-based video screens or computer terminals, push buttons, auditory feedback, flashing lights, or graphs and displays that visualize telemetry or logs.

An HMI is usually linked to the ICS's centralized SCADA databases to provide visualizations and metrics related to performance trends, diagnostic information, and other management parameters like maintenance schedules, infrastructure schematics, and technical information and manuals.

The HMI system usually presents the information to the operating personnel in the form of topology diagrams, allowing the operator to see a logical representation of the infrastructure. For instance, a schematic of a pump connected to a pipe can show the operator the pump is functioning and the amount of fluid flowing at a given time. The HMI may also allow the operator to not only visualize the infrastructure operation but also manipulate it through DCS type functions, in other words, adjust the flow rate of the pump in question. HMI visualization tools and capabilities may consist of topological diagrams, graphics, charts, dials, and any other engineering symbols or convention to represent process elements. It is even possible that images from closed-circuit television (CCTV) may be incorporated to allow operators to view the devices that are being monitored and manipulated.

Analogue versus IP Industrial Automation

ICS and process control systems are rooted in pneumatic or early forms of hydraulic controls. Originally, ICS used many forms of pneumatic (air pressure, steam pressure) or hydraulic (water or fluid pressure) to convey readings and send basic instructions around the infrastructure in question. Pneumatic control systems called for masses of tubes and many moving parts, which was expensive not only to deploy but also to move and maintain. When analogue systems based upon electronic waves transmitted through wires became available, the modern process control system was born and infrastructure owners rushed to adopt these systems; however, even now (2009) it is still possible to find pneumatic, hydraulic, and other legacy systems in use because they are so durable! Just because they were the first way of managing ICS does not necessarily mean they are immediately abandoned for newer alternatives, or were substantially inferior; but given a choice, these systems are increasingly more expensive options and not being deployed within green-field applications.

As a testament to the durability and reliability, consider some pneumatic systems implemented at the turn of the nineteenth century! Figure 1.1 shows pneumatic message delivery tubes. Put into operation in New York in 1897 by the American Pneumatic Service Company, the 27-mile system connected 22 post offices in Manhattan, and the general post office in Brooklyn as shown in Figure 1.2. At the height of its operation it carried some 95,000 letters a day, or one-third of all the mail being routed throughout New York City. The pneumatic message delivery system remained in service until 1953. Berlin had a similar system in use until 1976, while Paris and Prague use their pneumatic delivery systems to this day.[16] A variety of manufacturers of pneumatic message delivery systems continue to support and install these systems.[17]

From pneumatic systems, analogue ICS entered digital, but proprietary-digital rather than IP. A later push toward standardization

Figure 1.1 Pneumatic delivery tubes.

Figure 1.2 Pneumatic delivery tubes.

resulted in a variety of vendor-specific and later vendor-agnostic protocols that utilized various types of layer 1 physical media. These systems utilized a variety of purpose-built protocols designed for digital communications over analogue systems—like dial-up modems. Protocols such as Modbus, Distributed Network Protocol-3 (DNP3), ICCP, Profibus, and Conitel, to name a few, are process control-specific protocols intended for use over analogue communications carriers, such as the switched telephone networks of old using modems or even low-voltage wires running through an infrastructure. Additionally, some protocols such as Siemens H1 used traditional Ethernet media and networks, but utilized only partial implementation of the Transmission Control Protocol (TCP)/IP stack for fast data rates and service reliability. They often assumed that these technologies would not be converged with a traditional IT type network, and therefore did not need to be concerned as much with issues such as excessive multicast, or broadcast traffic interrupting communications.

Legacy ICS protocols were designed for very specific purposes and were not intended to be deployed for other applications or used in an open-systems context, where any vendor's devices would "speak" with any other vendor's devices. In fact, it was the opposite case in some instances; protocols were proprietary so that customers were locked into a vendor solution once the initial infrastructure was deployed. Because of their origin in slow, analogue carrier technologies, many of the earlier process control protocols were also designed to be "lite"—limited to what was needed to get the job done. As we will see, this has contributed to a significant threat to ICS security: the proprietary industrial protocols are vulnerable to attack and contain little to no inherent resiliency or security. Process control protocols were often functional but otherwise not well suited to the cruel world of modern IP networks.

The final step in process control network evolution after a move from analogue to digital is the evolution of digital to IP systems as the carrier/transport layer over a standardized IEEE 802.3 Ethernet data link layer. The move to IP was an obvious one for both manufacturers of ICS devices and systems and infrastructure owners. IP network equipment is ubiquitous and easy to deploy and support due to a large and readily available skills pool—not to mention cheap! IP also allows for the more efficient deployment of manufacturing intelligence, which in turn facilitate interfacing with IT business systems and visibility across the enterprise into the real-time nature and trends of production information. Such changes drive greater convergence and enable better, faster, and cheaper reporting, monitoring, and management for all elements of the infrastructure owners—not just the people in the plant. The movement of process control to IP is also an important component of a larger phenomenon in communication systems known as IP convergence.

Understanding IP convergence and its implications for communications security is an important element of understanding ICS security in this day and age because ICS is merely one of potentially several assets in the security profile of any modern network.

Convergence 101: It Is Not Just Process Data Crowding onto IP

Network convergence in relation to communications technologies has meant a variety of different things over the years, starting with a business strategy in the late 1980s that espoused a single supplier for television and telephony to consumers where the two services were traditionally separate and distinct businesses. However, the idea of mingling different types of communications content within the same network "pipe" is a relatively new definition of convergence that was spawned by the advent of Internet protocol IP—and the Internet—in the mid-1990s, but really only coming of age after the year 2000.

The most important thing to know about IP is that it has absolutely come to dominate the communications world of both voice and data. IP is a routing protocol that enables data from one network, for instance, an Ethernet network, to be directed to another (distant or local) network by either direct or circuitous paths. The Internet protocol, defined by IETF RFC791, is the routing layer datagram service of the TCP/IP suite or the transport layer of the OSI protocol suite. Figure 1.3 is a useful illustration of OSI versus TCP models and aids in understanding the reason of IP convergence given the market dominance of Ethernet for local and wide area networking.

The interconnectedness provided by IP (and supplemented by TCP, the primary error correcting/delivery assuring mechanism of the Internet) spawned applications like e-mail and file transfers, the original "killer apps" that drove Internet growth and IP adoption starting in the late 1980s. In the early 1990s the World Wide Web

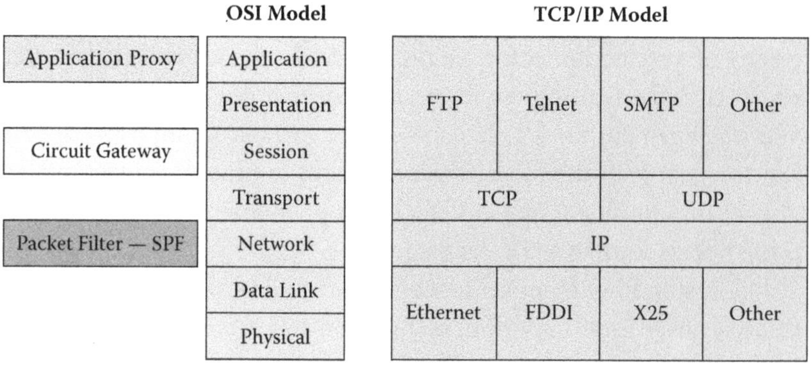

OSI Model		TCP/IP Model			
Application Proxy	Application	FTP	Telnet	SMTP	Other
	Presentation				
Circuit Gateway	Session				
	Transport	TCP		UDP	
Packet Filter — SPF	Network	IP			
	Data Link	Ethernet	FDDI	X25	Other
	Physical				

Figure 1.3 OSI layers versus TCP model. (From Gilbert Held, *A Practical Guide to Content Delivery Networks*, Auerbach, New York, 2006.)

(WWW) came along as the new killer app and popularized IP to the point of mooting other competing data routing standards, like X.400, for instance. In the ICS world it is now difficult to find a device made in the past few years that does not have some sort of HTTP interface for device health, configuration, monitoring, or other functions.

The result of this popularity is that IP networks, tools, equipment, and human skills became widely available and affordable and the IP networks grew to dominate not only interdomain network communications but intradomain communications—the IT applications for business LANs and wide area networks (WANs), voice applications, process control applications, and any other systems or services requiring reliable and cheap data transport.

Why did IP convergence take so long to arrive if digital ICS, cable television, telephones, and other data-oriented services have been in existence and overlapping since the 1980s? The reason convergence of these data assets did not occur earlier is that there was literally nothing obvious in terms of a common standard to converge onto. The introduction and rapid penetration of Internet services within business initially, but then to consumers starting in the mid-1990s, sped the emergence of IP as the clear and obvious winner of the network connectedness game, representing a beacon for all other communications technologies. There was suddenly something to converge toward, whether you were running the tried and true SS7 for switched telephony, or tied to an obscure, proprietary vendor protocol for ICS.

The business drivers to converge on IP were manifest for organizations of all sizes and consumers generally:

- Shared physical and logical networks reduce operational costs.
- Reduced/commoditized networking costs introduce new competitive imperatives in the market focused on features and applications (bells and whistles).
- New features and functions improved productivity and created wider choices for both lifestyle and work style.
- New varieties or service allowed more product flexibility within the legacy regulatory environment.

Each of these drivers of IP convergence will be discussed shortly. An immediate priority before getting deeper into this conversation is to clarify the definition of IP convergence and the sorts of infrastructure assets involved. Clarity around the nature of IP convergence will assist anyone dealing with ICS security because it provides vital context about the other information, communication, security, and safety assets that are paralleling ICS in migration to IP. Figure 1.4 is a nice depiction of the IP convergence phenomenon.

Convergence by Another Name

For the purposes of clarity it is worth mentioning that there are a few competing definitions of convergence in the world that could result in confusion for some readers. While these other forms of convergence are highly relevant, we are electing to focus on the issue of IP convergence, which is where the bulk of security impacts associated with convergence occur. Particularly, there is fixed-mobile convergence and cable-telecom convergence. Fixed-mobile is meaningful to our discussion because it has to do with ICS that were formerly restricted to fixed-line communications now adopting wireless. For instance, IEEE 802.15.4 (AKA Zigbee) is a low-bandwidth, low-power-consumption protocol designed specifically with home automation and ICS in mind. Similarly, the IEEE 802.11a/b/g/n (WiFi) protocols have become ubiquitous in all industries, and their application in ICS has become broad and deep. The other common form of convergence that is frequently discussed is more of a business as opposed to a technical concept: that of cable companies

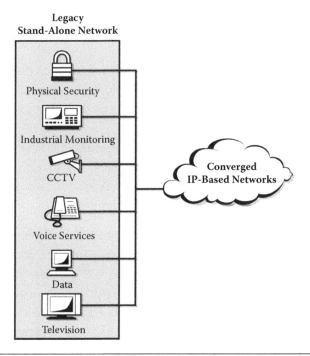

Figure 1.4 Assets converging onto IP networks. (From Tyson Macaulay, *Securing Converged IP Networks*, Auerbach, New York, 2006.)

getting into the "phone game" and telecom (phone) companies getting into the media and entertainment (cable) game.

Taxonomy of Convergence

Think of ICS, plus IT applications like e-mail, file transfers, the Internet, physical security and CCTV, and so on, as the primordial soup of communications technology, the biodiversity that is IP convergence. Convergence is not represented by a mathematically fixed number of applications or technologies. In fact, the number of eligible applications and technologies is forever growing. Possessing a high-level understanding of what technologies IP convergence is composed of, the questions of "When?" and "How serious is this?" is useful to gauge the imminence and severity of the ICS security issues covered by this book. What follows is a high-level taxonomy of some converging applications and technologies.

We can group the converging technologies under the following headings.

Triple-Play Convergence

The most obvious, contemporary example of IP convergence in the communications industry at large is called the "triple play"—Internet (data/IT), telephony, and entertainment (music/video) services all running on IP. The triple play is relevant to consumers and business alike. Voice-over IP (VOIP) represents the converged IP technology, with probably the most significant scope and scale to businesses. VOIP is the means of converting analogue sounds into digital packets for transmission over IP networks. In the case of VOIP, the mid-2000s marked the years when significant numbers of consumers started to adopt VOIP, with this number projected to reach 46%[18] of all broadband consumers by 2015. Large organizations are now moving in significant numbers to VOIP services and equipment. Similarly, entertainment and media applications like IPTV, movies, and music are projected to obtain significant market shares and become revenue-positive businesses only past 2012 or 2015. Entertainment and media products and services available over converged IP networks represent the conversion of mainstream analogue products and services to an end-to-end digital environment—delivered in packetized formats and transporting them to consumers over the same broadband Internet connection they currently get through broadband Internet connections. VOIP and entertainment and media in combination with IT services represent the triple play for telecoms carriers, which is seen as the current means to market victory.

Triple play consists of:

- IT services: This is the IP world of Internet and modern office systems. E-mail, file transfers, Web and Web services, online databases.
- Voice telephone: Voice telephony is packetized and placed onto routed IP networks. Voice mail systems are placed on the IP networks and calls may come and go from the Internet or out through gateways designed to interface with the traditional public switched telephone network (PSTN).
- Entertainment and media: Television channels and enhanced services—such as pay-per-view, movie, or music downloads—delivered on both a scheduled and on-demand basis.

Transparent Convergence

Transparent convergence is the movement of formerly proprietary and stand-alone networks, such as ICS, facilities management systems, and physical security systems, to IP. This convergence is almost entirely unobserved by anyone not closely involved with the management of these networks, but it has been ongoing since the late 1990s—as ICS first started moving to IP, with facilities management and physical security devices following shortly. Transparent convergence is therefore highly relevant to businesses owning and operating large physical assets or infrastructures, such as manufacturing facilities, buildings, rail networks, or pipelines.

As ICS user industries redeploy or upgrade process control elements to IP-based networks, transparent convergence gets underway. This book is a direct result of the transparent convergence of ICS to IP. Similarly, convergence to IP networking is also driving convergence to digital versus analogue information management and storage among all types of "transparent assets." In the case of physical security, digital video surveillance has supplanted analogue systems entirely in new deployments, with digital cameras replacing analogue cameras. In cases where it is a matter of retaining the older, expensive but higher-resolution analogue technology, it is a matter of converting the analogue information into digital formats and transporting it over IP networks to centralized digital video management systems. Like video, information and records related to physical access controls have moved entirely to digital formats in lock-step with transparent IP convergence: logs are stored in computers not printed out to long rolls of paper as they were only a few years ago. Therefore in the world of transparent assets like ICS, data in all its states of existence (in motion, at rest, in use) is converging on IP and digital formats.

Transparent convergence consists of:

- *ICS*—Remote monitoring and control of automation elements such as pumps, temperature gauges, and pressure levels.
- *Physical security*—Physical access controls on doors, CCTV for internal and perimeter surveillance, fire alarms and smoke detectors, motion detectors for burglar alarms, and public address and intercom systems.

- *Banking services*—Point of sale (POS) and automated banking machines (ABMs) for doing credit and debit transactions with merchants and increasing money transfers—and simply obtaining cash.
- *Facilities management*—Monitoring of facilities infrastructure for rapid maintenance, inventory management, and efficiencies. Control of heating and cooling systems, water systems, and electrical systems.
- *Metering*—Monitoring of endpoint usage by consumers of consumables such as energy, water, and parking spaces. The result is faster, more efficient, more flexible, and more accurate billing and troubleshooting.

Blue-Sky Convergence

Blue-sky convergence is the arrival of entirely new, IP-based functionality in existing goods and services, or the creation of entirely new goods and services based upon IP in the imminent future. Blue-sky convergence relies on technology and business concepts that are merely at the research stage, but seem intuitively viable and probable under the right social and political conditions. Unlike triple-play and transparent convergence, blue-sky convergence appears to be driven primarily by two major requirements: delivery of better and faster services from remote locations in order to increase a competitive advantage or simply maximize the amortization of expensive capital assets (whether they be software programs or super computers), and to allow scarce or expensive resources (such as service engineers, judges, or doctors) to be utilized as much as possible by eliminating downtime associated with travel and set-up-tear-down operations.

Blue-sky convergence is seeking the same business outcomes as triple-play and transparent convergence (improved efficiency and new, better features), but it goes one step further; it is seeking entirely new production and delivery paradigms. To end users, a phone is a phone, IP or not; the same for television, security cameras, ICS information, or water meters. Blue-sky convergence engenders not only a new delivery process, but an entirely new experience for the producer and consumer of the goods and services. In fact, blue-sky convergence really has little to do with convergence because an IP transport will be assumed by the implementers.

Blue sky consists of:

- Smart durables—Normal appliances like hot water tanks, fridges, stoves, microwaves, televisions, garage door openers, and so on, are embedded with simple network interfaces to access embedded systems for the purposes of in-field flaws remediation, license/warranty management, and remote control.
- Food and medicines are embedded with radio-frequency identifier (RFID) tags that possess network identifications (addresses) and can be tracked for inventory, regulatory, marketing, research, or other purposes.
- Smart roads, vehicles, airplanes, and railroads are injected with networked devices (strongly resembling ICS sensors) used to not only track but also control traffic flows and other process and safety-critical functions. Eventually IP addresses and simple diagnostic/remote control capabilities applied to lightbulbs and switches in buildings and perhaps fuel tanks and tires on fleet vehicles.
- Telepresence—The ability for people to (physically) engage in localized activities from remote locations. Telepresence has made incredibly rapid advancements recently, through seminal technologies like the drones used in theatres of war such as Iraq and Afghanistan during the 2000s. Airmen located in distant locations in Europe and North American fly combat missions and manage very real physical impacts thousands of miles away. While the nature of these communications technologies is not disclosed, it is almost certainly IP-based. But the real future of telepresence has yet to arrive and will include much more finite manipulation and control of remote environments; for instance, medical examinations or operations performed in disaster zones or battlefields by surgeons located safely behind the lines or on the other side of the world. Or a haircut and makeover from a famous Beverly Hills stylist and spa—but for a patron in Shanghai.

In the final chapter of this book we discuss the impact of the "Internet of things" and its relationship to ICS security.

The Business Drivers of IP Convergence

There are a variety of different business drivers associated with IP convergence—not just cost reduction. It is worthwhile to discuss the range of drivers as they may exist among all converging information and communication assets—and not limit our discussion to ICS business drivers. The benefit of a wider perspective for ICS managers and security practitioners is simple: better business cases for investment in ICS security.

IP convergence is enabled by a technological capability, but it is driven by a combination of market and nonmarket forces (demand and supply side controls). IP convergence is a matter of costs, competition, and regulatory legacy. Organizations need to offer goods and services to clients in a way that is better, faster, and cheaper than the competition. Regulatory drivers are inadvertent, and reflect market distortions introduced by government regulation, which actually propels convergence in unplanned ways.

Cost Drivers

If you think about IP convergence as a client or consumer of telecommunications services (as opposed to a provider, which most of us are not), the benefits of convergence are derived from:

1. Reducing costs associated with network management. Total cost of ownership is reduced through:
   - Reduced infrastructure—one physical network to maintain and amortized
   - Reduced staff and support costs for a common technology and network
   - Reduced moves, adds, and changes (MACs)
   - Reduced tolls and tariffs
   - Reduced costs associated with certification and accreditation of physical network components

2. Capturing new revenue streams through changing business models, especially in the area of entertainment and media where IP convergence is revolutionizing distribution and marketing for producers of content. Suddenly the old distribution and marketing channels of hard-copy VHS, CDs, or scheduled television with interruptive advertising are no longer the

only way to reach consumers. Not only that, but IP-based distribution and marketing tools also make old revenue centers like television advertising increasingly less efficient and effective, and provide revenue opportunities to those entities adopting converged technologies.

3. Increased productivity and efficiency within the user community by taking advantage of the newest features available to either clients or managers of the infrastructure. Gains can be realized through:

   - More powerful remote sensing and control of assets in ways never possible before the advent of cheap and fast IP-based networks
   - New "presence" applications associated with VOIP telephony that allow for targeted communications and less time spent "hunting" for individuals
   - The amalgamation of voice mail, e-mail, and fax to a single desktop interface
   - Data standards such as XML allow for different elements within the convergence network to use shared reporting and logging platforms—providing easily consolidated views and unified access control and archiving

4. Increased labor efficiencies:
   - Ability to monitor and control multiple assets or even multiple facilities across a geographically diverse area using a ubiquitous technology
   - Ability to respond to alarm and alert conditions more rapidly using overlapping procedures and diagnostic techniques
   - Ability to capitalize on localized experts supporting multiple areas efficiently

5. Better control of capital. Convergence allows organizations to have a single management interface to all the technologies engaged in the manipulation corporate information and assets (data, phone calls, manufacturing, HVAC, physical security, media consumption and provision)—generating positive impacts in the area of enterprise risk management:

- Reduced operational risks associated with control of intellectual property (technology, strategic/tactical market data), production processes, and communications
- Reduced financial risks associated with the control of sensitive regulatory (or regulated) data and the assurance of customer, partner, and internal data

6. Client pull. Device vendors in both the triple-play and transparent world are being forced to meet client demands for IP-based products. "The most significant change has been the evolving customer requirement for open architectures and commercial technology. Our customers wanted the flexibility to buy equipment from any automation supplier and have that equipment work in the multi-vendor environments that exist in most factories" (p. 8).[19] Telecom carriers are only mildly interested in transparent convergence because unlike telephony or television, the technology and services we have included as transparent are outside of either traditional carrier services or the traditional services of their bitter rivals—cable companies. Issues around customer retention and churn are not applicable.

7. Business continuity and disaster recovery. The start of the twenty-first century has seen event after event highlight the requirements for good business continuity (BC) and disaster recovery (DR) capabilities. But good BC and DR are expensive. Convergence offers the ability to reduce the costs associated with DR and BC because IP-based applications, systems, and processes and assets can be rerouted/redirected around failed network segments or facilities. Standard and highly reliable protocols like Open Shortest Path First (OSPF) and Border Gateway Protocol (BGP) offer the ability to automatically detect and reroute IP information to secondary sites (DR sites) where backup components can seamlessly assume the technical capabilities of information assets at costs that are far more affordable than historically possible. The net result is that development and support of high-availability capability and assurance for critical converged assets are attainable for more organizations and at lower thresholds. The cost of the safeguard relative to the losses associated with the risk (the

impact) has shifted and managers need to be aware of this shift. Managers need to revisit the costs associated with high availability under convergence and consider whether the cost of this type of assurance is still out of proportion to the potential losses/impacts; not doing so may produce uncomfortable questions from regulators or board members during the post-mortem associated with an outage.

Competitive Drivers

The potential to utilize a single, ubiquitous network technology such as IP has immediate impacts in the form of potential competitive advantages for adopters.

For those that own the networks within organizations, there is the savings to be accrued from running a single physical network and retaining a more homogenous technical skills set. For instance, the formerly separate physical wires for phones, IT, ICS, and facilities management can be converged to a single physical platform. While a single network may not be advisable, the fact that all systems are using an Ethernet platform means that more common equipment can be procured more cheaply and skills to maintain this equipment can be shared across departments. Previously, each department would have maintained its own human resources and applied distinct management systems to its own stand-alone networks.

For those that manufacturer devices for the various communications assets (voice, IT, entertainment and media, ICS, etc.) the ability to support a single network interface and specification drives costs down. Similarly, the fact that the network technology in question is well known and documented (IP) also means that the skills needed to deploy and manage the devices are in greater supply, reducing the barriers to market entry and customer adoption, versus the older, proprietary protocols and networks.

From a service provider's perspective—be they a telecom carrier or a cable company—the triple-play form of convergence is essentially about one thing: retaining or gaining customers. "Bundling has become more than a marketing tool; it is a necessary strategy for service providers to achieve three key objectives: acquire new customers, charge their current customers more, and retain their current customers."[20] Bundles also serve to actually reduce customer churn because customers are less likely to jump to a better offer the more comprehensively engaged they are with a supplier. This is critical for triple-play providers, as stand-alone, converged services such as VOIP and entertainment and media must exist in a highly competitive marketplace.

Regulatory Drivers

Regulation is intended to provide a balance between public interests and private interests and motives. Regulation in the ICS-User industries is renowned for being pervasive and pernicious, and there are regulatory elements in most national regimes that enable service providers to assertively push converged services onto clients. This phenomenon has been called de-standardization and is something that can impact the assurance of corporate communications and especially ICS security by provoking rapid migration from older telecom services to newly converged services. This migration often requires that endpoint devices be swapped for more modern solutions or that some form of network adaptor be placed in between the old device and the new network service.

De-standardization is the process by which telecommunications service providers are driving IP convergence through regulatory change requests. Part of telecommunication regulation is that tariffs have to be filed for all services and the setup and cession of telecoms services have to be approved. Service providers are actively seeking to redefine legacy services with regulatory agencies; this process is known as de-standardization. Service providers seek de-standardization because a particular service technology is no longer profitable; demand may have disappeared or it has simply been overtaken by better alternatives. As a result, the service provider makes an application to cease supporting that service under controlled tariffs because it would be losing money otherwise. De-standardization can mean two distinct things:

- That service providers no longer have to offer legacy telecom services (for instance, switched, low-bandwidth, low-yield services that process control systems might depend upon) at the same regulated tariff. Clients that wish to remain with legacy service can experience dramatic price increases once regulation is lifted. For owners of large, legacy process control services the result could be that maintaining older equipment under punitive tarrifs is more expensive than upgrading to IP-based devices and employing new, cheaper transport and network services.

- Carriers no longer have to offer the legacy service at all.

In either case, the ICS customer who may have found legacy services such as International Services Digital Network (ISDN) or Frame Relay to be perfectly adequate are pressed into a migration toward Digital Subscriber Loop (DSL), for instance. Another scenario impacting ICS is that tariffs on dial-up connections in remote areas suddenly become much more expensive as they are supplant with all-digital links; possibly the dial-up service is repriced to encourage adoption of cheaper to maintain wireless services? In any circumstance the migration is invariably converged toward IP solutions, because this is where the service providers are offering alternative services to supplant legacy services.

The lesson to be drawn is that telecommunications regulation is something that businesses assume will benefit them, but of which they have little understanding. Legacy services are often maintained due to regulatory edict far past the point at which their margins have become unacceptable from a business perspective. This is an instance of contradiction between intent and outcomes of regulation: without regulation, a service provider would slowly raise the price of a legacy service to maintain margins and force attrition in the service. Businesses would move from the legacy service to newer, cheaper services at their own pace, according to the relative financial burden of the gradual cost increases. With regulation, and the de-standardization process, businesses may experience a whiplash as service providers abruptly increase the costs of legacy services or simply cancel services. At that point businesses are forced to make rapid decisions about the critical communications services that can impact the assurance of their organizational telecommunications significantly.

The Conflicting Priorities of Convergence

Convergence should not be thought of as merely placing more applications and services on the same network; convergence must also be considered from the perspective of the enforced aggregation of all the data and communications priorities resulting from a shared IP medium. This translates to the convergence of not just the assets, but the sensitivity of these assets too.

Complicating the nature of security for all assets under convergence is that different converged assets have different requirements related to the assurance trinity of confidentiality, integrity, and availability. The orthodoxy of network security is that assurance requirements must satisfy the most sensitive asset on the network in the areas of confidentiality, integrity, and availability. Security is a matter of the strongest requirements, not a matter of averaging. Figure 1.5 shows how this assessment approach would be applied in the context of e-mail services on an IT network.

Figure 1.5 displays the emergent behavior associated with converged IP networks, where a new and heightened sensitivity arises that can exceed the sensitivity of any of the component assets. In other words, the whole becomes greater than the sum of the parts. Consider the example of a large infrastructure operator that has implemented (for a variety of good reasons) an IP network that supports its IT services (business data), process control services, and voice services. While these assets might

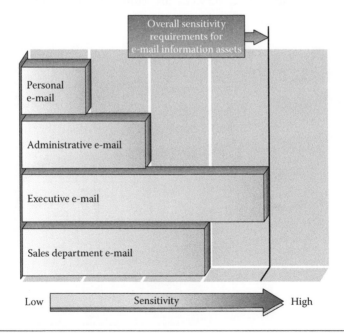

Figure 1.5 Sensitivity assessment of mixed assets. (From Tyson Macaulay, *Security Converged IP Networks*, Auerbach, New York, 2006.)

have been kept logically separate (on different network addresses and subnets), they may very well share a few common elements, such as wiring closets, UPS devices, and probably network operators. These distinct assets might even share certain network elements, such as switches, routers, or firewalls. If something happens to threaten any of these shared elements, then all the assets are at risk. Therefore, the value of the shared elements will actually exceed the value of any single assets since the loss of these elements can mean the loss of all assets.

ICS Security Architecture and Convergence

The fundamental reason behind the emergence of ICS as a priority domain for security practitioners is the phenomenon of the traditional ICS architecture converging with modern IT architecture due to the dominance of IP and Ethernet technologies. ICS security architecture is not the intended topic of this book or chapter; however, we will address it briefly in this section because of its potential impact on security assessment practices.

Figure 1.6 depicts a traditional ICS architecture within an enterprise environment. ICS services are running on isolated networks

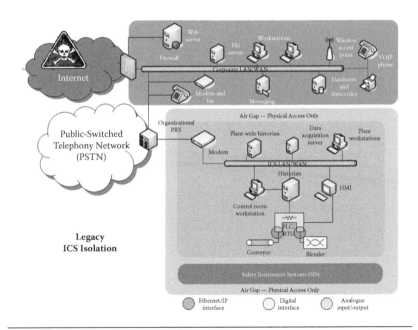

Figure 1.6 Legacy ICS architecture.

(air-gapped), and use industrial protocols directly at layer 2 of the network stack, such as Modbus or Profibus. Reports from the ICS environment used for management purposes would have to be generated on the ICS devices and manually transported to the corporate network devices. Alternately, raw data could be extracted from the ICS devices to be input into corporate devices for processing and reporting. The safety instrumented systems were also air-gapped from both the ICS and the corporate networks. The ICS networks have always had logical connections to the outside world in the form of modem banks used for remote access by vendors. Direct, day-to-day vendor (manufacturer, supplier, integrator) support for ICS devices and systems is much more common than in the IT world, where consultant and internal staff do most maintenance, rather than the manufacturers. For this reason, most, if not all, ICS will have modems used by manufacturers and suppliers to update, troubleshoot, and sometimes manage the ICS directly. Additionally, the vendors making connections often do so using specialized software that utilizes the proprietary protocols of the manufacturer directly.

Figure 1.7 shows a modern, converged ICS network, where the corporate network interfaces directly to the ICS network. The business

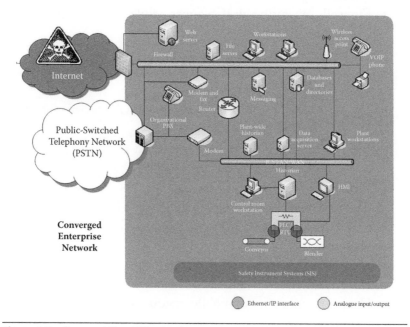

Figure 1.7 Converged IT and ICS networks.

advantages of this are substantial: reporting and production monitoring are greatly enhanced, cost of network equipment and administration declines, product alternatives become available as everyone speaks IP. This architecture shows that the interface between corporate networks and ICS networks can occur in a variety of ways. Interconnection can be through network elements such as routers (or switches or firewalls), or through multihome devices (devices with two or more Ethernet interfaces). Figure 1.7 also shows how the ICS and SIS may reside on the same physical IP network, sharing elements such as routers and switches. Not shown is segregation between the ICS and the SIS that might typically consist of network address translation (NAT) if not a layer 3 or layer 4 firewall implementation of varying degrees of sophistication.

The ICS architecture displayed in Figure 1.7 is demonstrative and does not reflect the espoused best practices for ICS security architecture from entities such as ISA, NIST,[21] or the UK Centre for Protection and National Infrastructure.[22] Distinct best practices in the area of ICS security may include:

- Zoning of both the corporate and ICS networks, with putative filtering and change management on ICS zones
- Firewalls separating all ICS zones, while routers might separate corporate zones
- No multihomed devices
- Network monitoring for rate-based vulnerabilities on the ICS network
- Distinct network access controls and AAA services for corporate and ICS
- Data diode services allowing only read privileges from the corporate to ICS assets
- Virtual terminal services for vendors and support staff to prevent direct machine-to-machine communication from remote sites
- Telephony firewalls to prevent voice lines from being used for modem calls
- Upstream (carrier cloud-based) security to detect malware and bot infections
- Heavy restriction on mobile media on the ICS devices (USB, floppies)

The Discussions to Follow in This Book

Chapter 2 will seek to discuss in greater detail the types of threats that might face an ICS infrastructure—how they are different from threats facing IT service infrastructure but also how they are the similar.

Vulnerabilities are what threats take advantage of in order to compromise assets, ICS or otherwise. Chapter 3 focuses on ICS vulnerabilities. The type of vulnerability affects the likelihood that a threat will be successful in an attempt to compromise, and this is half the formula behind risk: the likelihood of a threat being successful. The other half of that formula is the severity of the resulting impact after the assets have been compromised, taking into account existing controls and safeguards.

Chapter 4 is a discussion of some new and developing approaches for assessing ICS risks and planning remediation strategies based on quantitative metrics and evidence, versus professional opinion and intuition. Chapter 4 will review a widely understood safety concept in ICS—the safety integrity level (SIL) and its application in existing management systems and processes. We then move on to introduce an evolving concept known as security assurance level (SAL) as the counterpart of the SIL metrics. Chapter 4 will also expose a novel application of a well-known manufacturing management tool: overall equipment effectiveness (OEE). Methodologies of applying OEE to security assessment and business case development will be proposed. Finally, Chapter 4 will investigate evolving threat assessment techniques and technologies available beyond the ICS network into carrier environments, and powerful if not mandatory adjuncts to any ICS security assessment process in the future.

Chapter 5 is about what is next for ICS security issues, and focused on developments related to the IP networks underlying ICS, rather than new forms of ICS itself. These developments in IP will be so fundamental as to incredibly expand the potential definition and scope of practice for ICS security practitioners. Many of these changes are occurring behind the scenes in ways that most people are unaware of, and the effects will start to appear in the (still) fragile ICS environments within a matter of months to a couple of years, without a doubt.

Endnotes

1. http://csrc.nist.gov/publications/PubsDrafts.html and http://www.cpni.gov.uk.

2. http://www.cert.org.

3. http://www.pcsforum.org. The U.S. Department of Homeland Security (DHS) Control Systems Security Program (CSSP) has established the Industrial Control Systems Joint Working Group (ICSJWG). This group supersedes the Process Control System Forum (PCSF), which was disbanded.

4. http://www.ferc.gov/.

5. http://www.nerc.com.

6. http://www.nrc.gov.

7. http://www.dhs.gov.

8. http://www.whitehouse.gov/news/releases/2003/12/20031217-5.html.

9. http://www.gao.gov/htext/d071075t.html.

10. *Symantec—Internet Security Threat Report—Trends for 2010*, http://www4.symantec.com/.

11. Kevin Yoo, *A Glimpse into Delphi: The World's First Industrial Cyber Security Vulnerability Database*, Wurldtech Security Technologies, Vancouver, 2009, http://www.wurldtech.com.

12. Gartner Research, *The M2M Market Evolution: Growth Attracts Everyone*, June 2011.

13. DHS SCADA Security Procurement Language for Control Systems, http://www.us-cert.gov/control_systems/pdf/SCADA_Procurement_DHS_Final_to_Issue_08-19-08.pdf, and U.S. CERT, http://www.us-cert.gov/control_systems/.

14. NTSB pipeline accident report, http://www.ntsb.gov/Publictn/2002/PAR0202.pdf.

15. Ibid.

16. Curious expositions, http://curiousexpeditions.org.

17. See http://www.capsu.org/library/small_diameter_manufacturers.html.

18. IDC Market Analysis, *Canadian Consumer Voice, Internet, and Wireless Services 2011-2015 Forecast*, May 2011.

19. Rockwell Automation, Annual Report, 2008, p. 8.

20. Bundles: Beyond the Triple Play, *RHK Insight*, November 2004.

21. National Institute of Standards and Technology (NIST) 800-82, *Guide to Industrial Control System Security*, 2008.

22. UK CPNI, Process Control and SCADA Security, http://www.cpni.gov.uk/Products/guidelines.aspx.

2
THREATS TO ICS

Many of the people reading this book will be acquainted with the concepts of threats, vulnerabilities, and risks, and how they relate to each other. However, to be sure that we are all speaking the same language, a review is in order. Threats are either human based or natural in origin. A threat agent is the actor or active force that generates a specific threat; it could be organized crime or mother nature. Understanding threat agents facing you and your assets is distinct from merely understanding the threat, and enables better mitigation strategies. Understanding the source of threats and the assets they are directing their efforts against is a form of "intelligence" in the cloak and dagger sense of the word. Many organizations have limited visibility or intelligence about threats generally, and therefore little insight into the threat agents, their motives and methods, and the types of assets they may target. Without such information, treating threats becomes uncomfortably close to guesswork.

This is particularly true in industrial settings where a physical process that is easily observable and interacted with is coupled with a mystery of digital communications and software logic to control the process. Specifically, industrial asset owners are accustomed to solving the physical problems of the process with the mechanical and electrical engineering practices that have traditionally supported these processes, and are unaccustomed to associating intentional threats to the control systems within a live running process. This disconnect results in a false perception that the physical process is free from cybersecurity threats.

In this chapter we become specific about threats and threat agents, who they are in the context of industrial control system (ICS) security, how they work, and what their objectives and motivations are. We will attempt to do this using a combination of fully cited opinions from reputable sources, empirical observations, and plain old opinions. Far from being definitive, the list of threats that we present reflects only the information available to the authors at the time of writing; this information can optimistically be considered indicative of the real-life range of threats aligned against ICS. No one can or ever will possess a comprehensive and detailed list of all threats; we just do our best. Vulnerabilities are what threats take advantage of in order to compromise an asset, ICS or otherwise. Chapter 3 focuses of ICS vulnerabilities.

Threats to ICS: How Security Requirements Are Different from ICS to IT

It is always useful to establish a level platform from which to build your ideas and discussions. In this case we started in Chapter 1 with a discussion of the distinction between IT security and ICS security in terms of confidentiality, integrity, and availability. While there are many similarities, there are also differences that are critical to the process of threat, vulnerability, and risk assessment.

This section will outline at a high level these security requirements to frame the discussion to follow related to specific threats and threat agents. As NIST 800-82 puts it:

> ICS have many characteristics that differ from traditional Internet-based information processing systems, including different risks and priorities. Some of these include significant risk to the health and safety of human lives, serious damage to the environment, and financial issues such as production losses, negative impact to a nation's economy, and compromise of proprietary information. ICS have different performance and reliability requirements and use operating systems and applications that may be considered unconventional to typical IT support personnel. Furthermore, the goals of safety and efficiency can sometimes conflict with security in the design and operation of control systems (e.g., requiring password authentication and authorization should not hamper or interfere with emergency actions for ICS).

Table 2.1 is drawn directly from NIST 800-82 and reproduced here in order to provide a continuity of perspective and terms rather than presenting the reader with alternative and possibly confusing and redundant discussion about the distinctions between IT and ICS from a security perspective. Initially, it had been our intent to generate purely original content related to this topic of ICS sensitivity, but upon

Table 2.1   Distinct ICS Security Requirements and Sensitivity

REQUIREMENT	DESCRIPTION
Performance	ICS are generally time critical; neither delay nor jitter is acceptable for the delivery of information, and high throughput is typically not essential. In contrast, IT systems typically require high throughput, but they can typically withstand some level of delay and jitter. ICS must exhibit deterministic responses.
Availability	Many ICS processes are continuous in nature. Unexpected outages of systems that control industrial processes are not acceptable. Outages often must be planned and scheduled days/weeks in advance. Exhaustive predeployment testing is essential to ensure high availability for the ICS. In addition to unexpected outages, many control systems cannot be easily stopped and started without affecting production. In some cases, the products being produced or equipment being used is more important than the information being relayed. Therefore, use of typical IT strategies such as rebooting a component is usually not an acceptable solution due to the adverse impact on the requirements for high availability, reliability, and maintainability of the ICS. Some ICS employ redundant components, often running in parallel, to provide continuity when primary components are unavailable.
Risk management	In a typical IT system, data confidentiality and integrity are typically the primary concerns. For an ICS, human safety and fault tolerance to prevent loss of life or endangerment of public health or confidence, regulatory compliance, loss of equipment, loss of intellectual property, or lost or damaged products are the primary concerns. The personnel responsible for operating, securing, and maintaining ICS must understand the important link between safety and security.
Architecture security focus	In a typical IT system, the primary focus of security is protecting the operation of IT assets, whether centralized or distributed, and the information stored on or transmitted among these assets. In some architectures, information stored and processed centrally is more critical and is afforded more protection. For ICS, edge clients (e.g., PLC, operator station, DCS controller) need to be carefully protected since they are directly responsible for controlling the end processes. The protection of the central server is still very important in an ICS, since the central server could possibly adversely impact every edge device.
Physical interaction	In a typical IT system, there is not physical interaction with the environment. ICS can have very complex interactions with physical processes and consequences in the ICS domain that can manifest in physical events. All security functions integrated into the ICS must be tested (e.g., offline on a comparable ICS) to prove that they do not compromise normal ICS functionality.
	(Author's comment: Modern access control systems often combine physical and logical controls together into a single solution. Increasingly, physical security controls are fusing with IT systems and physical interaction is a definite reality of IT security assessment and planning.)

(Continued)

Table 2.1   Distinct ICS Security Requirements and Sensitivity (Continued)

REQUIREMENT	DESCRIPTION
Time-critical responses	In a typical IT system, access control can be implemented without significant regard for data flow. For some ICS, automated response time or system response to human interaction is very critical. For example, requiring password authentication and authorization on an HMI should not hamper or interfere with emergency actions for ICS. Information flow must not be interrupted or compromised. Access to these systems should be restricted by rigorous physical security controls.
System operation	ICS operating systems (OS) and applications may not tolerate typical IT security practices. Legacy systems are especially vulnerable to resource unavailability and timing disruptions. Control networks are often more complex and require a different level of expertise (e.g., control networks are typically managed by control engineers, not IT personnel). Software and hardware applications are more difficult to upgrade in an operational control system network. Many systems may not have desired features, including encryption capabilities, error logging, and password protection.
	(Author's note: This seems to be closely related to the previous availability distinction, but with more elitist overtones. Elitism among ICS practitioners is still common and contributes to the problem of ICS versus IT, not the solution. See comment below related to change management.)
Resource constraints	ICS and their real-time OS are often resource-constrained systems that usually do not include typical IT security capabilities. There may not be computing resources available on ICS components to retrofit these systems with current security capabilities. Additionally, in some instances, third-party security solutions are not allowed due to ICS vendor license and service agreements, and loss of service support can occur if third-party applications are installed without vendor acknowledgment or approval.
	(Author's note: This condition is also very true for many IT systems, especially in large enterprises were strict service levels must be supported. Many vendor solutions related to applications and services do not support anything but approved vendor patches. Often patches are never approved even though vulnerable operating systems are being employed. ICS do not face this condition alone.)
Communications	Communication protocols and media used by ICS environments for field device control and intraprocessor communication are typically different from the generic IT environment, and may be proprietary.

Table 2.1 Distinct ICS Security Requirements and Sensitivity (Continued)

REQUIREMENT	DESCRIPTION
Change management	Change management is paramount to maintaining the integrity of both IT and control systems. Unpatched systems represent one of the greatest vulnerabilities to a system. Software updates on IT systems, including security patches, are typically applied in a timely fashion based on appropriate security policy and procedures. In addition, these procedures are often automated using server-based tools. Software updates on ICS cannot always be implemented on a timely basis because these updates need to be thoroughly tested by the vendor of the industrial control application and the end user of the application before being implemented, and ICS outages often must be planned and scheduled days/weeks in advance. The ICS may also require revalidation as part of the update process. Another issue is that many ICS utilize older versions of operating systems that are no longer supported by the vendor. Consequently, available patches may not be applicable. Change management is also applicable to hardware and firmware. The change management process, when applied to ICS, requires careful assessment by ICS experts (e.g., control engineers) working in conjunction with security and IT personnel. *(Author's note: This condition is really only true on desktop computers or possibly within small business. Enterprise applications and systems that form the backbone of industrial economies suffer from similar constraints. Patching and updates are a highly controlled process involving extensive tests that reveal flaws and bugs in patches that result in more risk than keeping the systems unpatched.)*
Managed support	Typical IT systems allow for diversified support styles, perhaps supporting disparate but interconnected technology architectures. For ICS, service support is usually via a single vendor, which may not have a diversified and interoperable support solution from another vendor. *(Author's note: Major vendors of IT solutions such as IBM, Cisco, Oracle, or SAP do not have any integrated form of support either. Managed support is just as much a challenge for large enterprise IT systems as ICS: vendor conflicts cause no end of trouble in IT environments.)*
Component lifetime	Typical IT components have a lifetime on the order of 3 to 5 years, with brevity due to the quick evolution of technology. For ICS where technology has been developed in many cases for a very specific use and implementation, the lifetime of the deployed technology is often in the order of 15 to 20 years and sometimes longer.
Access to components	Typical IT components are usually local and easy to access, while ICS components can be isolated, remote, and require extensive physical effort to gain access to them.

Source: National Institute of Standards and Technology (NIST) 800-82.

the release of 800-82 in the summer of 2008, it became apparent that there was more value in building upon National Institute of Standards and Technology's (NIST) work, rather than competing with it.

In some instances we have seen fit to apply annotations to the NIST definitions that expand or clarify the work. In the author's notes in Table 2.1 we will challenge some conclusions about the differences between ICS and IT security, where they appear to lack perspective or perhaps unhelpfully echo "us versus them" sentiments, which can be observed between ICS and IT security practitioners from time to time.

As was the case with ICS security requirements, we have elected to reproduce the NIST comparison of IT versus ICS requirements verbatim so that we could have the opportunity to comment further. The NIST work is excellent, but more could be done to reconcile the ICS and IT communities. Both these communities will be brought closer and closer together in the future as a matter of IP convergence; there is substantial benefit in understanding similarities in the area of threats and risks as well as differences.

Table 2.2 derived from NIST 800-82, further exposes the fact that IT security and ICS security are related but distinct practices, imposing on the security practitioner the requirement to carefully balance requirements at interface points or on shared network platforms. This is especially true in environments that are actively practicing IP convergence on the network assets: where ICS data are being mixed and mingled with IT data on the same physical devices and wires, even if the data are (supposedly) logically separated by virtual local area networks (VLANs), switching, and a range of other techniques. Examples include varying degrees of network and physical separation including:

- Totally converged IT and process control network (PCN) communications.
- Logically separated IT/PCN environments that apply no ingress or egress filtering beyond simple access control lists (ACLs) to PCN traffic, separated by technical controls such as simple packet filtering firewalls or virtual LANs (VLANs).
- Firewall isolated networks with strong PCN ingress filtering (and limited to no egress filtering), with the firewall as a simple edge networking device.

Table 2.2 Summary of IT Security and ICS Differences

CATEGORY	INFORMATION TECHNOLOGY SYSTEMS	INDUSTRIAL CONTROL SYSTEM
Performance requirements	Nonreal-time response must be consistent High throughput is demanded High delay and jitter may be acceptable *(Author's note: This is simply not true. IT systems in banks are every bit as real time as ICS. This also ignores the ongoing and widespread migration to VOIP at the enterprise level as well as domestically. Twenty milliseconds of latency also make a conversation unintelligible.)*	Real time Response is time critical Modest throughput is acceptable High delay or jitter is not acceptable
Availability requirements	Responses such as rebooting are acceptable Availability deficiencies can often be tolerated, depending on the system's operational requirements *(Author's note: Similar to the performance requirements comment: availability on many IT systems, especially converged systems, is critical. Banking and telephony applications are merely two examples.)*	Responses such as rebooting may not be acceptable because of process availability requirements Availability requirements may necessitate redundant systems Outages must be planned and scheduled days/weeks in advance High availability requires exhaustive predeployment testing
Risk management requirements	Data confidentiality and integrity are paramount Fault tolerance is less important— momentary downtime is not a major risk Major risk impact is delay of business operations	Human safety is paramount, followed by protection of the process Fault tolerance is essential; even momentary downtime may not be acceptable Major risk impacts are regulatory noncompliance, environmental impacts, loss of life, equipment, or production
Architecture security focus	Primary focus is protecting the IT assets, and the information stored on or transmitted among these assets	Central server may require more protection Primary goal is to protect edge clients (e.g., field devices such as process controllers) Protection of central server is also important

(Continued)

Table 2.2 Summary of IT Security and ICS Differences (Continued)

CATEGORY	INFORMATION TECHNOLOGY SYSTEMS	INDUSTRIAL CONTROL SYSTEM
Unintended consequences	Security solutions are designed around typical IT systems *(Author's note: Enterprise-grade applications and systems are put through multiple layers of testing and "soak" before deployment. Telecommunications and banking apply no less rigor than any ICS asset manager, and possibly more in some cases.)*	Security tools must be tested (e.g., offline on a comparable ICS) to ensure that they do not compromise normal ICS operation
Time-critical interaction	Less critical emergency interaction Tightly restricted access control can be implemented to the degree necessary for security *(Author's note: Largely true for pure IT but not the case for converged assets such as telephony of physical security controls, like fire alarms and emergency intercoms in parking garages.)*	Response to human and other emergency interaction is critical Access to ICS should be strictly controlled, but should not hamper or interfere with human–machine interaction
System operation	Systems are designed for use with typical operating systems Upgrades are straightforward with the availability of automated deployment tools *(Author's note: Not for high-availability enterprise systems. Autoupdate will frequently break vendor warranties.)*	Differing and possibly proprietary operating systems, often without security capabilities built in Software changes must be carefully made, usually by software vendors, because of the specialized control algorithms and perhaps modified hardware and software involved
Resource constraints	Systems are specified with enough resources to support the addition of third-party applications such as security solutions	Systems are designed to support the intended industrial process and may not have enough memory and computing resources to support the addition of security capabilities
Communications	Standard communications protocols Primarily wired networks with some localized wireless capabilities Typical IT networking practices	Many proprietary and standard communication protocols Several types of communications media used, including dedicated wire and wireless (radio and satellite) Networks are complex and sometimes require the expertise of control engineers

Table 2.2   Summary of IT Security and ICS Differences (Continued)

CATEGORY	INFORMATION TECHNOLOGY SYSTEMS	INDUSTRIAL CONTROL SYSTEM
Change management	Software changes are applied in a timely fashion in the presence of good security policy and procedures. The procedures are often automated *(Author's note: Not for high-availability enterprise systems. Autoupdate will frequently break vendor warranties.)*	Software changes must be thoroughly tested and deployed incrementally throughout a system to ensure that the integrity of the control system is maintained ICS outages often must be planned and scheduled days/weeks in advance ICS may use OS that are no longer supported
Managed support	Allows for diversified support styles	Service support is usually via a single vendor
Component lifetime	Lifetime on the order of 3 to 5 years	Lifetime on the order of 15 to 20 years
Access to components	Components are usually local and easy to access	Components can be isolated, remote, and require extensive physical effort to gain access to them

Source: National Institute for Standards and Technology (NIST) 800-82.

- Advanced firewall with De-Militarized Zone (DMZ) technology where the DMZ is used as a managed zone to share network information with the PCN, or a more enhanced architecture with both strong ingress and egress filtering.
- "Air gapped" network where there is either no electronic communications between IT and PCN, or all electronic IT to PCN communications are served across non-IP or other routable network communications (such as serial).
- Combinations of the above.

Threat Treatment in ICS and IT

Adding to the discussion above is the differing traditional approach to threat treatment between ICS and IT security—IT security solutions often approach security challenges by adding another piece of software to the devices to support security or possibly another device to the network (FW, IDS/IPS). This approach does not translate well to the ICS world, and in many cases is simply not technically possible. Not possible given the design of the ICS devices, which are specifically fit for the purpose of reliable (versus secure) performance in a production process. These components are often designed to handle physical stresses such as heat or moisture common to many process control environments, and highly reliable in terms of hardware failures under normal operating conditions. From a security resilience perspective, few possess sufficient capacity to host additional security processes and may not respond well to intermediary, in-line devices that may add latency to time-critical process instructions, particularly in the realm of safety instrumented systems (SIS). Add to this the possibility that ICS devices and networks may have been custom designed, and the addition of nonnative security elements may break vendor warranty. Alternately, the ICS itself may be so old and fragile that it simply will not tolerate new and invasive security assets that even slightly alter the operating environment. A typical plant environment often includes a veritable museum of automation within the architectures, as the components are designed to be operational for 12 to 15 years, or as many as 30, before the process is decommissioned or completely upgraded.

Threats to ICS

Are ICS threats distinct from IT threats? And can they be considered as distinct as the security requirements themselves? The answer is basically no. Similar threat agents target both IT and ICS assets, but the difference for the authors is that ICS is more likely to suffer as a matter of the "lucky hit" or collateral damage, as opposed to a direct attack. Given that most ICS processes are multifaceted architectures involving multiple disparate systems, and often compensating controls such as SIS, a maximum damage attack scenario against a modern ICS plant is extremely complicated. This is not to suggest it is not possible, quite the contrary. But, this complication does assist in the identification and classification of threat agents.

In this way, ICS faces a duel threat: a direct threat through the loss of control of the compromised ICS devices (primarily Windows-based devices), to the point that any ICS control, monitoring, or recording operation performed by that device can be executed, interrupted, cancelled, delayed, or changed by the new masters; and an indirect threat

Table 2.3 ICS Threat Agents

THREAT AGENT	PROFILE	TARGETED ASSETS
Professional bot herders	Like malware wholesalers. They invest in the development and management of bot herds, and then rent them out to any of the other threat agents.	Seek to gain control of devices in order to repurpose them on demand and rent or sell the herd to any and all of the other agents.
Organized crime	Gangs and crime syndicates, engaged in debit and card fraud, now find that chip-based technology is forcing them online for better returns.	Personal identity information for identity theft and multiple forms of fraud. Personal banking information.
Industrial espionage	Mercenary type entities hired to target specific corporate assets and industries.	Intellectual property, financial, and production information, plans, and strategies.
Foreign intelligence services/ nation-states	State-sponsored entities, possibly paramilitary, usually operating from identifiable networks or geographic regions, if you can trace them.	National secrets, plans, and strategies, and industrial secrets, plans and strategies.
Spammers	Specialize in harvesting legitimate e-mail addresses from sources such as Web sites, blogs, social networks, Web mail providers, and any other possible source. Generate massive lists of addresses, both real and randomized/ guessed to send junk e-mail (spam).	Individuals who will either buy (semi)legitimate products ("organic Viagra"), submit to fraudulent transactions, identity theft, or pyramid schemes, or fence stolen goods.
Phishers	In close effort with spammers, phishers attempt to attract individual users to Web sites loaded with malicious software in order to compromise the user devices once they connect to a Web site, and gain access to contents or make them into bots.	Individual fraud and identity theft, industrial espionage as described above, and public sector entities for national security assets.
Activists and terrorists	Ideologically motivated entities typically without the resources to develop exploits independently, but with enough resources to hire compromised devices from herders or leverage off-the-shelf exploit "kits."	Industrial sabotage of assets (physical or logical), public sector entities, and government and military for planning, strategic, or national security secrets.

of impacts associated with the probing, scanning, and attacking that inadvertently impacts fragile ICS devices.

Table 2.3 is a simple overview of cyber the prime types of cyber threat agents and the assets they typically target. Many threat agents are, in effect, a composite of several of the categories defined in Table 2.3, operating under several profiles according to where the opportunity for profit lies. The network elements and what reveal the threat agents are described and discussed in depth later in this chapter.

At a simpler level, threat-from[1] entities in the specific context of ICS security might be divided by insiders versus outsiders, and targeted versus collateral impacts. Many of the threat agents identified as separate entities are in fact converged threat agents—they have adopted similar techniques and related objectives to the point that they may appear to be acting as one attacking agent. Differentiating between phishers, spammers, foreign intelligence, and organized crime is not very productive if they are all using the same attack vectors.[2] Understanding the threat agent is useful for the typical ICS environment, but focusing too much on this classification has, in our experience, shown to take very valuable time away from identifying threat vectors, and in fact may cause many threat vectors to be erroneously ignored altogether.

Table 2.4 outlines a simple framework for considering threats against ICS. Starting from a simpler list makes decisions about which ICS controls and safeguards to employ just a little bit easier. The columns of the table represent insiders versus outsiders: insiders are employs, contractors, or others with specific, trusted access to resources and information from the ICS asset owner; outsiders are everyone else, including those that may specifically target ICS and

Table 2.4 ICS Threat Matrix

	INSIDERS	OUTSIDERS
Targeted impact	Threats using internal resources from within the security perimeter by privileged, trained users	Threats through compromised security perimeter followed by a compromise using ICS-specific skills and tools deliberately acquired
Unintended impacts (lucky strike)	Threats from within the security perimeter on interconnected systems (financial, HR, network assets) for other purposes (malicious, foolish) cascade into ICS and generate impacts and compromises	Threats through the security perimeter compromise non-ICS assets (servers, desktops, laptops) and cascade impacts to ICS components either by spawned "child" attacks or infrastructure interdependences (bandwidth, switches, routers, Dynamic Host Configuration Protocol [DHCP] services, etc.)

those that simply target any asset utilizing IP and network access. The rows represent either impacts targeted at ICS assets deliberately or impacts that occur as a result of collateral damage, or a direct impact that happens as a matter of chance or coincidence.

Threat-To and Threat-From

At the highest level, there are two distinct variants of threat: threat-from and threat-to. Threat-from is about the threat agent and the resources and characteristics of a given agent. At the coarsest level some threat-from information is free and widely available from sources like the Computer Emergency Readiness Team (CERT), McAfee, Symantec, Counterpane, and plenty of others. These sources may provide information about some of the agents currently active in the world, for instance, the country that is the apparent source of the most attacks, types of organizations, or individuals launching attacks (attempting to exploit exposures such as the virus of the day, worm of the day, phish of the day, software vulnerability of the day, patch of the day, and general bogey man of the day). This type of public domain threat-from information is of limited value because it does not contain specifically actionable intelligence. Ideally, threat-from information will contain detailed metrics such as apparent network of origin, organization of origin, estimated resources available to the agent, such as money, skills, and time, motivation of the agent, and objectives of the agent. This sort of threat-from information is strategic in nature, not tactical: it will provide intelligence about the likelihood of success, and the expected force, velocity, and duration of exploitation attempts. For ICS security practitioners concerned about specifically identifiable assets in identifiable locations, threat-from information, whether specific or accurate, is hardly actionable.

Table 2.4 has a specific limit for understanding threats generally, and possibly ICS threats specifically: it deals entirely with where the threat is coming from (threat-from information), which is how IT security typically deals with threats for two specific reasons. First, threat-from information is easier to manage. It tends to be less precise, often purely qualitative: "threat level orange" or "organized crime." Therefore threat-from is easier to consume and assimilate, but because it can often be unactionable, it is also easier to ignore. Second,

IT assets are typically spread broad and deep across an organization and are often unclassified. Personal information, intellectual property, strategic plans, and financial statements often flow unchecked through organizations and reside in many locations they have no reason to appear within. Identifying which data assets are under threat and where these data lie is extremely difficult with open networks and the current generation of security tools. Therefore, again, threat-from information can be difficult to action but easy to ignore for IT security practitioners. While the first point applies to ICS practitioner equally, the second does not. ICS are more identifiable assets, and their data are generally not to be found scattered. This means that threat-from information can be more readily assessed technically, by observation.

Threat-to is asset-specific, whether the assets are logical (information, systems, or networks) or physical (buildings, plants, infrastructure). Like threat-from information, coarse threat-to information is also publicly available from sources such as the Department of Homeland Security/Public Safety Canada, Information Sharing and Analysis Centers (ISACs), and a variety of other open sources. These sources may provide information about which industries or sectors appear to be experiencing exploitations more than previously observed. For instance, some of the most granular information related to publicly available threat-to is about financial losses year over year. Again, this type of public domain threat-to information is of limited value because it does not contain specifically actionable intelligence. Ideally, threat-to information will contain detailed metrics such as asset ownership, asset names and locations (physical and logical), asset role, asset interdependencies, asset valuation, and business impact assessments. This sort of threat-to information is rare, never in the public domain, and highly sought after by industry; it is highly tactical and can support detailed response and remediation, especially when combined with detailed threat-from information. Good insight from threat-to metrics will provide intelligence about the potential level of impact. For the ICS practitioner this may be insight into the systems and network interfaces being probed, attacked, and penetrated, or it may be the physical infrastructure that is being targeted and therefore the logical interfaces with this infrastructure that need increased diligence.

While much of this chapter will discuss threat-from observations and analysis, the chapter will also increasingly deal with threat-to intelligence sources and how they might be employed by ICS security managers.

The Most Serious Threat to ICS

Making prescriptive statements about things as dynamic and ethereal as a threat can be hazardous and professionally irresponsible. But here we go anyway: given today's network threat environment, ICS security impacts are first and foremost likely to occur as a result of unintended effects of outsider attacks.

ICS are being specifically targeted by threat agents, at least that is what the security analysts say. Yet, the chances of a random hit from sophisticated attack vectors employed by a converged threat population are greatest. "Random" in the sense that semi- or fully automated malware, in a quest for data with monetary value, stumbles upon and impacts ICS. This means that while the determined intentional attacker scenario is valid and should be integrated as part of a risk management program, the typical ICS operator should focus much more on the day-to-day sustainability and survivability of its components from the chance threats that are likely to occur. What makes us so certain about this?

In this next section we are going to discuss the most insidious threat on the Internet today: computer hi-jacking for the purposes of hosting botnets, spam relays, phishing sites, and other forms of "malware"—as in "malicious software." This threat is not specific to ICS, but it is essentially the embodiment of all of the ICS adversaries enumerated by NIST. Computer hi-jacking for the purposes of bots, spam, phishing, and malware is the purview of organized crime and foreign intelligence services taking advantage of system vulnerabilities and exploit tools that have been purpose built from scratch. These are the infamous zero-day exploits/vulnerabilities that pass through firewalls and antivirus systems because the vendors have never detected them previously, therefore mooting the ability to generate signatures; these exploits are significant investments for organized crime and foreign intelligence agencies, and they are not published or disclosed for glory like the archetypical hacker would do in the "old days" (1990s).

Collateral Damage

The largest generalized threat to ICS security is related to collateral damage from systems that have been hi-jacked for the illicit purposes of organized crime and foreign intelligence. The ICS assets can be directly targeted through attacks on ICS support systems: management consoles running standard operating systems, service laptops, file servers, or desktops attached to the ICS network. But ICS can also be indirectly targeted through attacks on systems within interconnected business networks. The premise of the indirect attack is that while the ICS network may be too difficult to reach remotely, it is a much softer target from an internal network. Like layered defense, layered attack methodologies become appropriate when targeting ICS networks.

Threat agents may not necessarily directly target PLCs, remote terminal units (RTUs), or supervisory control and data acquisition (SCADA); they may target devices in the network proximity of ICS that are running vulnerable operating systems and applications, and have these devices launch attacks on everything in the vicinity. These entities will have varying degrees of interest in ICS, probably foreign intelligence more so than organized crime since the kinetic impacts often associated with ICS compromise wreak havoc and destruction but not necessarily cash, the way a compromised banking account might.

The following section discusses the nature of specific attack and compromise methodologies (tradecraft), which are launched by outsiders and are likely to inflict collateral, if not direct, damage on ICS.

Whatever Happened to the Old-Fashioned E-Mail Virus?   In the good old days e-mail viruses and worms were effectively mitigated through security software on the desktop or e-mail server. Those days are gone. The days when a well-configured router could become a firewall are also gone. In days gone by, malware on the Internet was largely intended to wreak havoc and win glory for the purveyors—"juice" for whoever coded the sublime attachment that suckers millions of people into opening it and destroying their own systems. This is no longer the fashion. While malware is still being coded for no other reason than to destroy data and inflict harm on the (mostly) innocent victims, this is perceived as a waste of perfectly good skills in an age where millions of dollars are being made by organized crime through malware propagation and hi-jacking systems to steal banking passwords, identities, and to use as pawns in massively distributed attacks.

What many people—ICS security managers included—are less aware of is that the days of effective and trustworthy application-based firewalls are also gone. The new generation of malware is highly sophisticated and not announced by the authors in order to garner the associated fame and notoriety among peers. It is kept as secret as possible, as long as possible, by the owners and creators. The current generation of malware is also designed to morph and change itself on the fly to prevent detection and even appear unrelated to itself as it propagates and spawns sons and daughters. This is not the virus and worm of your youth.

In the U.S. state of Florida they say that you should assume that any body of water that you cannot see to the bottom of has an alligator in it, and you should take precautions with your children and pets. The same should be said about any IP network in the face of the new and evolving threats on the Internet. If it is an IP network, assume that something nasty will crawl in there one evening and act accordingly.

Do not believe that any IP network is truly isolated because it is not; the notion of a completely disconnected system has never been observed by the authors—no matter that the ICS network may have multiple security zones and perimeter firewalls with IDS services and network access controls. Something always remains that provides communications paths, both inbound and outbound, that can facilitate the loss of information, spread of malware, or other threats. The Stuxnet virus found in 2010 is a great example of this in that one of its deployment mechanisms involved using USB thumb drives to spread the attack and "jump" network perimeters.

If a threat is "zero day" in nature, then compromised devices are not recognized as such by security systems. Any device that interconnects intermittently with other networks—like a laptop—is a potential agent of infection. Similarly, USB sticks, portable hard drives, and cell phones/smart phones with available and accessible memory are all extremely difficult to control and present Trojan horses into most networks and security zones.

Money, Money, Money

The objective of malicious computing in 2011 and beyond is not to smash data and grab glory; it is to accumulate and hoard control over massive populations of compromised computers and turn these devices to the bidding of their masters for profit.

Profit from the control of these hi-jacked systems comes in many forms. First, there is the money that can be defrauded from the individual owners as their banking data are stolen and personal wealth drained away through a variety of online techniques involving identity theft, cash transfer, stock trades, credit card balance transfers, and so on. Second, and related to number one, is the ability to compromise corporate intellectual property and sell to the highest bidder—or simply use it for your own industrial purposes (espionage). Third, there is the ability to sell the services of the compromised computers for illicit purposes such as spam e-mailing, illegal site hosting, and distributed denial of service (DDOS) attacks. Fourth, hi-jacked systems may be rented or tasked out through "piece work" in deliberate attempts to compromise ICS (for state-sponsored terrorist or foreign intelligence) or other networks. These are four high-level reasons for malicious entities to invest in the development of new, sophisticated, and (at least initially) undetectable types of computer compromises and malware. But there is a fifth significant reason to hi-jack systems. This reason is particular to ICS: to trigger kinetic impacts in the real world.

The Fatally Curious, Naïve, and Gullible

The ways and means to become infected by malware increase every day and are more cunning every day. Traditionally, malware might be something that is picked up from installing questionable software from questionable sources—often related to song lyrics, celebrity images, gambling, games, pirate software, and porn. This software might be downloaded from a Web or FTP site on the Internet, but increasingly it is distributed through file sharing systems such as Bittorrent, eDonkey, and Gnutella.

In the context of threats to ICS, it is very common for corporate assets (desktops and laptops) to be used for personal pursuits. In most enterprises, this is even permissible within "reasonable limits" under the security policy. In this manner, corporate assets are infected as insiders download a file for personal use on what they believe to be a temporary basis, intending to delete the file from the corporate machine afterward. This file might be a popular but expensive software application (think Adobe Photoshop) that will appear to install well enough but will be bundled with the malware. Once installed, the malware cannot easily be removed even with sophisticated tools. Another means of planting malware through downloaded files is by taking advantage of hooks within media players such as Windows Media player that allows Web sites to be spawned from video files; once a browser is open, a variety of bogus screens and prompts limited only by human imagination can be mimicked to try and convince people to download and install malware—even though the video file that started it all is otherwise benign.

This is a form of social engineering and is now one of the most effective and pervasive manners in which to propagate malware. In the old days, social engineering was considered a resource-intensive and risky task because it involved one person communicating directly with another person (often on the phone) and tricking him or her into revealing information through impersonation and acting skills. Social engineering also involved significant knowledge of inside processes and systems so that the threat agent could appear to be legitimate in its requests. Some of the earliest and most successful hackers took advantage of telecom carrier networks by gaining privileged network access through social engineering: they sounded like telecom engineers trying to fix arcane network problems—and needed information, privileges, and passwords. They were successful because they had learned the carrier's internal processes and the obscure industry-specific protocols that ran the networking prior to IP communications. This allowed them to bluff information from employees. This is not the social engineering of today.

The social engineering of today takes advantage of the myriad contemporary social networks and communications tools: chat and messaging services such as Facebook and My Space, blogs, and Twitter. The way social engineering is accomplished today is to compromise a social network account (through a compromised desktop or simply through sloppy passwords) and then leverage the trusted social connections associated with that account to infect other machines, for instance, compromised machines with active MS Messenger services and active accounts with buddy lists.[3] Once this social asset is detected by modern malware, it will push messages to everyone on the buddy list under the username of the person who uses the compromised device. With something like "LOL [laugh out loud] ... cleaning my file system and found this picture of you! http://www.youshouldknow-better.com/naked.pif," because the message is ostensibly from someone known, the victim is more inclined to click through and become infected. Once infected, all buddies/contacts/friends/whoever will get similar baiting messages. This exact scenario has caused no end of grief for all the social networks and is a soft underbelly for malware propagation, hitting new social networking services as fast as they are launched. This particular threat is not likely to diminish in the near future because part of the value proposition of social networking is to have relatively open systems that allow personal outreach; throwing up walls reduces the efficiency of this process.

Hi-Jacking Malware

Most of the threat taxonomies associated with ICS, including sources such as NIST 800-82, boil down to hi-jacking malware and the implied botnets. The primary authors and controllers of this malware, as discussed previously, are various forms of criminals and foreign intelligence services. All the "adversaries" NIST discusses in 800-82 with the single exception of "insiders" revolve around hi-jacking malware. This actually makes the discussion of threats to ICS a little easier to manage because we have a single focal point from which to start; namely, what is hi-jacking malware and why does it threaten ICS?

Most malware is based upon vulnerabilities found in Microsoft-based operating systems (Windows) and popular software packages that tend to run on Windows. Other operating systems, such as Macintosh OSX and Linux (with probably less than 10% the desktop market between them[4]), have a proportionally lower incidence of reported malware vulnerabilities and resulting threats. Figure 2.1 shows the ever expanding population of malware.

To the extent that ICS control and visualization consoles, historians, and interconnecting enterprise resource planning (ERP) systems are Windows-based, they are directly threatened by botnet malware

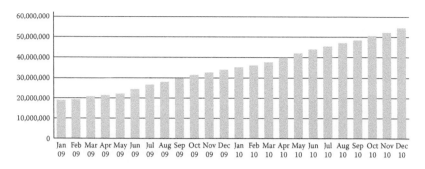

Figure 2.1 Total malware samples in the database. (From *McAfee Threat Report—Fourth Quarter 2010*.)

attacks that slip silently through perimeter security, either through Web-based exploits or on portable storage devices like USB keys, personal media players, or smart phones.

Even if the ICS devices are not based upon Windows operating systems, they can certainly suffer from the collateral damage if a Windows device in their proximity becomes infected. Similarly, in the course of performing its automated reconnaissance, modern malware will scan all reachable networks: if there is even the smallest hole in a firewall or error in a routing or switching table leading to the ICS network, modern malware will find it.

Part of the threat we are about to discuss is directly related to the fragility of ICS, and how the brute force seek-and-attack nature of modern malware has an unintended, lethal effect.

How easily is malware slipping past perimeter security? Consider a few facts from testing by independent third parties on the effectiveness of antivirus software. Figure 2.2 shows the effectiveness of various antivirus (AV) software solutions on newly identified malware. This means that they tested the software against novel (less than 2 weeks old), incoming malware with an updated signature base of the AV software. The results show that even the best vendor will allow 40% of malware to pass undetected, and the worst will allow 90% to pass undetected.[5] Given that signature bases contain millions of signatures from the preceding two decades of AV development, the only explanation of the results is that even with freshly updated signatures, lots of malware flows right past these security controls. What applies for AV solutions will also apply to application-level firewall and deep

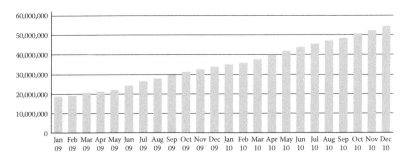

Figure 2.2 Novel malware detection rates. (From AV-Comparisons.org, May 2010.)

packet inspection intrusion detection systems (IDS) and intrusion prevention systems (IPS) because they by and large come from the same vendor community and are drawing upon related sources and signature bases as the AV software.

To reinforce the meaning of these results in Figure 2.2, the test criteria were for previously identified malware (past 2 weeks), with signatures developed. In the case of completely new, unique, novel, or proprietary malware built by entities such as organized crime, terrorists, or intelligence agencies, it should be assumed that almost 100% of such malware will pass perimeter security undetected for significant periods of time. In fact, malware creators are known to actually test and modify their malware to ensure it is undetected by AV products prior to releasing it into the wild: tools for this purposes are freely available on the net for testing suspect code for viruses, but these same utilities can just as easily be used to test that malware is not detected.[6]

There is another way around antivirus systems that might be deployed within networks adjacent to ICS: compromising a corporate DNS server and waiting for AV services to perform autoupdates on their signature files. DNS attacks are some of the most potent and difficult to deal with on the Internet because the infrastructure is simple in concept (associate human-readable domain names to IP addresses), critical (because the most popular services like e-mail and Web services utterly fail without it), and administratively complex (take a look at a complete DNS record for a moderately size enterprise with "nslookup type=any yourdomain.com"). Frequently DNS services will be attacked and compromised, but left largely functional by the attackers. Because the basic functionality of DNS is pretty simple to most users, a compromise can remain undetected. A compromised DNS server can then send users and their semiautomated services to bad places by supplanting the IP address of the legitimate destination with a malicious IP address hosting a malicious service. Compromised DNS servers have been known to send security software to the wrong servers for bogus updates—forcing them to download malware along with signature libraries.

So why especially are the antivirus and malware recognition systems missing so much? First, much of the malware will arrive on systems in a packed format—compressed, obfuscated—which is different from how it looks once it is unpacked on the system and running. By varying the obfuscation in simple manners, it flies through detection systems, and by the time it assumes a form that is consistent and recognizable, it is too late. Additionally, many malwares will immediately disable AV and host IDS software as the first order of business once installed. Postinstallation, malware may revert to its packed/obfuscated format and nestle deep into the file system by setting (s)ystem, (h)idden, and (r)ead-only attribute flags on its files. Many AV solutions skip files with these flags set.

Even more threatening to ICS assets (and IT assets generally) is the insidious ability of modern malware to morph itself during its breeding cycle. This code will actually rewrite its children in various ways such that they are unique and distinct and will evade detection, even if the parent is found out and a signature released.

Similarly, it may be tempting to ignore the smart phone or other mobile devices as they proliferate; these devices are becoming more prevalent in ICS environments. IP network or Bluetooth-enabled devices are supported by many ICS vendors for use in interacting with process control equipment, and network communications mediums such as Global Packet Radio Service (GPRS), and EDGE (3G cellular) are commonly used in widely distributed ICS environments (such as in intelligence meters used for smart grid, water quality monitoring stations, and similar remote sites). Figure 2.3 shows how mobile-specific malware is now being tracked as a unique entitiy, representing a very real and new threat vector.

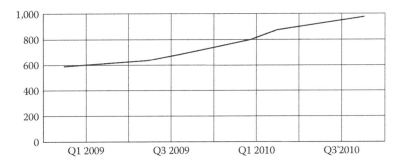

Figure 2.3 Mobile malware growth by quarter. (From *McAfee Threat Report—Fourth Quarter 2010.*)

No Room for Amateurs

Increasing the likelihood of a direct strike on Windows-based ICS systems or collateral damage on fragile ICS networks and devices, is the professional competition that has come to permeate the malware industry. Strongly indicating this intense competition in the malware design and maintenance business is the growth in fake security products. These products do, in fact, remove malware, but only the malware of the competing botnet owners, leaving "friendly" malware to prosper. See Figure 2.4 for the rapid growth in fake security software.

Taxonomy of Hi-Jacking Malware and Botnets

We stated earlier in this chapter that hi-jacking malware and its various masters is essentially what NIST identified as the top adversarial threat to ICS, and we concur. Hi-jacking malware is an evasive, highly

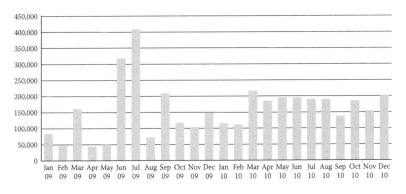

Figure 2.4 Fake security software detected. (From *McAfee Threat Report—Fourth Quarter 2010.*)

tooled, and malicious piece of software implanted into (typically) a Windows-based device that enables services and information on the device to be triggered or accessed by remote entities. It also transforms the compromised device into a platform for cascading threats that can have serious direct and indirect impacts on ICS.

Direct impact is through the loss of control of the compromised devices to a third party, to the point that any ICS control, monitoring, or recording operations performed by that device can be executed, interrupted, cancelled, delayed, or changed by the new masters. The indirect impacts associated with modern malware and botnets relate to the modus operandi to be discussed immediately: automated probing, scanning, and attacking that inadvertently impacts fragile ICS devices.

Hi-Jacking Malware 101

We are now going to review and discuss several categories of hijacking malware to expose their tradecraft, mode of operations, and objectives. This information is useful in the context of ICS security because understanding how modern malware operates is the first step in toward controls and safeguards to counter these threats, which are most likely to penetrate the security perimeter and zones undetected to result in ICS impacts. None of these forms of hi-jacking malware is specifically directed or intended to attack ICS services; however, variants on these forms have been found to target certain industries and critical infrastructure sectors, such as defense and finance. There is no reason to believe that ICS-specific targeting has not or could not be deployed through such malware. But regardless of whether or not modern malware is targeted at ICS, it is potentially lethal.

The types of hi-jacking malware we will cover include:

- Bot (drone/zombie)
  - Socks4/Socks5/HTTP connect proxy
  - Simple Mail Transfer Protocol (SMTP) spam engine
- Porn dialers (dial-up/FAX modem, and IPT)

Characteristics of a Bot (Zombie/Drone)
Bots are the endpoints in the increasingly familiar botnets that make the security headlines more and more. Bots are the primary

form of modern hi-jacking malware threatening ICS security. They encompass the range of malware we will discuss in this section as an umbrella term. Bots are sometimes referred to as zombies or drones because they mindlessly do the bidding of their controllers regardless of what is in their own interest. A collection of bots under the control of a single herder is the eponymous botnet.

Bots are in part characterized by their ability to maintain their command and control (C&C) communications channels with their owners/herders. These channels are critical to making the bots fully functional and revenue-generating resources, since C&C enables a the range of activities and instruction sets, such as the spamming and attacking we will discuss below. Bots use fully qualified domain names (FQDNs) for understanding where to direct C&C requests. Using FQDNs allows bot herders to move control locations around dynamically to avoid detection and to give the C&C network a high degree of resilience from disruption (as long as control over a compromised domain is maintained).

Using the C&C channel, the bot herder will have the ability to change not only the FQDN of the control servers, but also other tell-tale indicators, such as the port used for communications, plus or push upgrades to the bot software and even make the bot go dormant. All of which are very useful in avoiding detection by network-based security countermeasures, such as IDS and IPS services. Making this process of compromise and control more difficult to trace and detect is the increasing use of encryption in the C&C channels, denying many forms of intrusion detection and intrusion prevention from observing traffic that has no business in the network. More will be discussed on this in Chapter 4.

A common C&C channel employed between bots and their masters involves the Internet Relay Chat (IRC) protocol and IRC servers, but increasingly the Hypertext Transport Protocol (HTTP) (Web) is used because this enables control traffic to mix and mingle with legitimate HTTP traffic on the LAN, enterprise network, and Internet. (IRC is not a common protocol for business or average, everyday users, and therefore is more suspiciously obvious within a corporate environment.) Both protocols are capable of supporting payload (file) delivery, and thus the use of IRC and HTTP means that anything can also be downloaded through the C&C channel and executed on the compromised device. This makes it possible for mere worker bots to be "promoted" into C&C bots to control other bots and to provide the redundancy of C&C within the herd, which has been known to grow into millions of compromised computers in the single herd![7] For instance, a bot master may download an IRC or Web server (HTTP) to a bot, set up and configure this server to retrieve commands upstream, and relay them downstream to other bots who are instructed to receive commands from the newly installed server. By this system of C&C networks within C&C networks, if a bot master loses some of the C&C servers, new ones are ready to assume the duties.

Whether used as a C&C relay or not, once a computer is turned into a bot, it can be put to work by searching for valuable information on the compromised devices and all the attached drives, scanning for other devices to compromise on the local network, or searching for file systems and storage networks for assets such as intellectual property. If such information is found, it may then be transmitted back to the designated controller or a drop point (another compromised device) specified by the controller. In such circumstances, the impact on the compromised device and the network it inhabits can be substantial, as large amounts of bandwidth are suddenly consumed. For fragile ICS services, this can present a critical problem, described further in Chapter 3.

It is also possible that bots could be set to search for special devices to attack on the local networks, such as ICS devices. Instructions of this sort can be easily sent from bot herders through their C&C channels to possibly hundreds of thousands of devices at the same time. Even if the bot herders do not really have the knowledge and wherewithal to try and compromise or control ICS devices, it is a simple enough matter to issue bot instructions to flood the local networks with traffic to create denial of service attacks from within the security perimeter. Similarly, botnets have become so large and extended that bot masters do not really know where they are specifically. Instructions and tools specific to ICS can be deployed to hundreds of thousands or even millions of devices at once—just hoping for a hit!

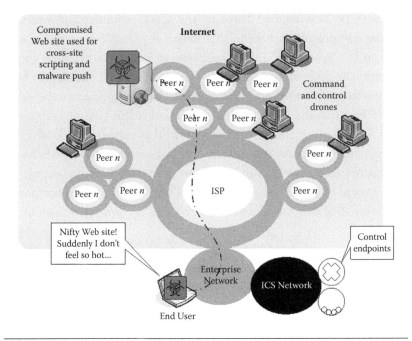

Figure 2.5 Malware infection.

The Reproductive Cycle of Modern Malware

Understanding the tradecraft associated with modern malware is essential to understanding its threat to ICS. Figure 2.5 shows a device being compromised by malware that is delivered through a cross-site scripting attack that passes undetected through firewalls on HTTP port 80. Alternately, the malware payload could be delivered through more mundane means like an infected USB memory stick or an Office Suite document. In this example, the user's browser is directed to a link on a compromised Web server that pushes malware up to the user and displays bogus prompts, like "free virus scan," which the user clicks and approves. Typically, these links are found within sites offering song lyrics, celebrity photos and gossip, free trials of gambling or porn, and bogus charities, but require the user to allow an otherwise prohibited activity on his or her computer to get access. Naturally, the activity appears benign but actually results in the compromise. Malicious links are also embedded within the Web pages of legitimate sites if the servers have been compromised. In this way the downloaded application, script, or activeX control appears to come from a trusted source.

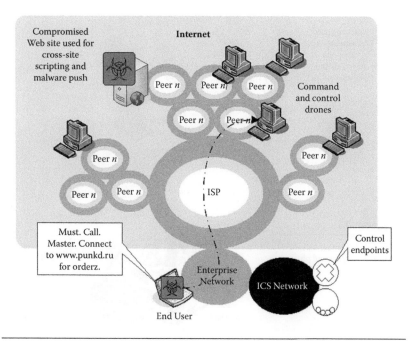

Figure 2.6 Compromised device registers with the herd.

Figure 2.6 shows the next stage of compromise immediately after the malware has been downloaded and installed on the target device. Once installed, the malware will do a number of things, such as reset its own file permissions so that it is essentially invisible without special computer forensics tools. Under the command of the malware, the infected device then connects to a FQDM that has been configured by the malware author; this connection may be through IRC channels on high ports, employing peer-to-peer protocols, or as is increasingly common, through HTTP sessions on standard ports. The benefit of using HTTP is that these connections can pass right through corporate proxies and firewalls as apparently legitimate traffic. This first connection is to announce the birth of a new bot (slave) to the herd and to receive configuration details about where to go for instructions in the future if a different FQDM is to be used for redundancy purposes.

Once fully enrolled in the botnet, the bot herder (not shown in diagrams—they are buried deep behind the scenes using multiple layers of C&C drones to relay instructions) uses the command and control drones to push instructions and commands or download and

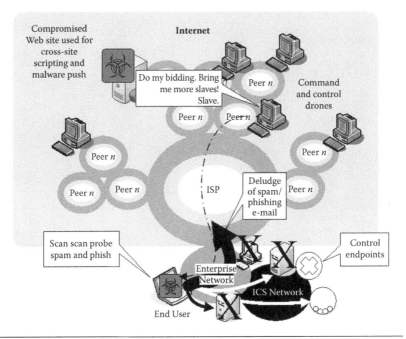

Figure 2.7 Compromised device receives and executes bot controller instructions.

run software. Figure 2.7 shows the communications arriving through HTTP communications, which pass seamlessly through firewall and antivirus technologies. In this instance the compromised device may be instructed to act as a spam engine, pushing thousands of messages a second out the local network using the enterprise resources. Alternately, the bot could be programmed to search for specific types of devices and assets according to any characteristics visible through network fingering printing: ports, protocol implementations, OS signatures, MAC address manufacturer, and more. The resulting impact on the network and the infrastructure elements can be devastating, not just due to the outbound traffic, but the related bounces from bad e-mail/IP addresses (backscatter) and blacklisting from major message exchanges and partners.

In Figure 2.7, the compromised device is ordered to commence a scan of the local IP range looking for other potential victims, and then start port tests on any responding IP addresses. As can be imagined, such practices can bring a LAN segment to its knees quickly, and if a few other machines are infected in the process, an entire enterprise network can be brought down through the resulting denial of services, which may not even be an intentional act by the bot herders! This is the sort of collateral damage to a network that can pose extreme threats to ICS, even if they happen to be logically segmented but sharing some network elements such as routers, switches, DHCP, directory, or DNS services. Similarly, any ICS devices that happen to be sensitive to scans and probes (fragile) may find themselves facing a sustained flood of these activities, as multiple internal devices are compromised and repeat the same pattern.

The process illustrated in this series of diagrams applies pretty much across the range of hi-jacking malware, even though the example used for the purposes of this discussion has been botnet controllers. Besides the potential to infect other computers on the network and supplant their intended operations with illicit operations, bots can have devastating effects on the network infrastructure itself, beyond those mentioned related to port scans and backscatter. For instance, in the course of performing sequential, rapid scans of the local and adjacent subnets, a large number of Address Resolution Protocol (ARP) requests can be generated. These ARP requests are known to rapidly degrade switch and router memory and load CPUs to the point of failure. Similarly, older Cisco routers utilize "IP prefix caching" for fast switching; when faced with rapid port scanning, they can cause the IP cache to grow to such a large size that memory depletion occurs and causes the router to malfunction. This problem has been addressed in newer routers through an alternate method of IP prefix caching called Cisco Express Forwarding (CEF), but old routers, as might be found in aging ICS networks, using the vulnerable IP caching (fast-switching) technique still exist. In the case of ICS network deployments with long life spans, it is possible that the network vulnerably posed by botnets and other hi-jacking malware is even more serious than might be the case for more modern IT networks, which will generally replace network elements entirely every 4 to 7 years.

Other sorts of malware that can have dire impacts on an ICS network by nature of their operating mode include Socks proxy, SMTP spam engines, and porn dialers. We will briefly review these forms of hi-jacking malware so that their unique operating modes and traits become more recognizable to ICS and IT security practitioners.

A Socks 4/Sock 5/HTTP Connect Proxy

Socks stands for sockets, as in port sockets used in TCP protocol communications over Internet protocol (IP). A Socks proxy will accept connections on TCP ports and relay them outward to the intended destination. An HTTP proxy does the same thing, but only for the Hypertext Transport Protocol (HTTP), the application protocol of the World Wide Web.

The first thing hi-jacking proxy malware will do after it is successfully installed on a compromised device is employ one of various techniques to call home and register its availability, the most frequent means of which involves a HTTP transaction toward a specialized control server. This control server is not generally a msaster server with any direct connection to the actual, human owners—it is just one in a series of cascading control points as discussed earlier. These control servers may be hard coded within the malware registration mechanism using a fully qualified domain name (FQDN), usually also under the control of the human owner, but possibly a domain name of a legitimate entity that has had its domain name management system compromised. Using a FQDN (e.g., badsocks.fruitcompany. za) allows the human owner to move the control server dynamically (by simply changing the IP address the FQDN resolves to) or add additional IP entries to support additional available control servers for load sharing or scalability purposes in larger proxy networks. A benefit of this control architecture is that in the event a control server (which is just another hi-jacked computer in all likelihood) is taken offline because the owner figures out it is compromised, all traffic can be quickly redirected to other sources. Even in the event that the control server is not discovered by the actual computer owners, regular changes of the FQDN may still be undertaken by the "owner" of the Socks proxy to reduce clues and remain stealthy.

The first step in the life of a hi-jacked proxy will be a test. The new owner will test the services that will be subsequently employed and probably rented out to entities such as professional spammers and phishers. For instance, the control server will immediately sent an SMTP (e-mail) message through the (Socks in this case) proxy to test the functionality; if the message gets through, then the hi-jacked machine is functional and can be immediately rented or sold as a functional asset.

The whole process of registration, testing, and utilization/renting of a S4/S5/HTTP proxy can happen in a matter of minutes since it is all automated. And to put a cherry on the whole thing, some of the more sophisticated hi-jacking malware will check the various open-source security sites on the Internet from time to time to see if their new proxy's IP address has been flagged and placed on a spam list. If this is the case, the Socks service can be discontinued before the owner notices, and control maintained for other purposes—or to just wait until the IP address is removed from the open-source lists.

And what about the actual system owner of the hi-jacked computer with the Socks proxy? What are they doing throughout this process and what might they see? If the user of the machine is interacting with the computer while it is busy performing illicit tasks for the nefarious controller, they will immediately notice a degradation in performance. The hard disk will spin incessantly and CPU utilization will be 100% for no apparent reason. There is no limit to the number of reasons that a user might tolerate this performance; often they just figure its a short-term issue associated with automated patching, or perhaps just beyond their control deep in the guts of the systems. In the case of a system performing critical processing or operations, it is entirely possibly that processing delays will occur. Similarly, data streams into the compromised device will experience increased loss and processing errors as the operating system struggles to manage the load. In the instance of ICS, this data loss or corruption could present significant threats, beyond what many data-centric systems might experience.

If the compromised system remains online and hi-jacked for a significant period, the user will find that his Internet service provider or network administrator will contact him demanding an explanation for his abusive network usage; this will be shortly followed by more annoying consequences, such as blacklisting of his IP space (cut off by parts of the Internet) and of course public humiliation by being put on open- source abuse lists like Spam and Open Relay Blocking System (SORBS)[8] or SpamHaus.[9] These consequences are problematic for any organization because of the interruption in business communications. But for organizations relying on the Internet to provide access to important remote operators or suppliers providing support, this may be especially critical.

To the extent that an ICS is supported through VPNs using the Internet, the support service provided through these VPNs may also become unavailable. Unavailable because the hi-jacked systems are consuming so much bandwidth, and also because ISPs start to deny or throttle traffic for domains on the blacklist and drop traffic from compromised IPs because they pose a threat to the larger upstream networks. Realistically, ISPs will not quickly blacklist another ISP or IP address within the same country or even from a reputable international carrier; however, many foreign carriers and ISPs will not be granted much leniency. If ICS data feeds are coming from remote locations in less developed or stable parts of the world, these locations, if compromised by hi-jacking malware, might find themselves rapidly blacklisted and cut off from HQ. Therefore the threat to remotely operated ICS in far off places is potentially greater than local ICS, because connectivity could be completely severed by the local service providers!

SMTP Spam Engines

SMTP engines are similar in nature to the Socks proxies discussed above, but rather than relaying spam mail messages from other sources, these engines will fetch the intended message text and a (massive) address list and create the message from scratch on the machine. Once the message has been formatted and prepared, the engine will start initiating connections to the local SMTP servers defined in the computer configuration for legitimate enterprise e-mail applications, therefore consuming not only the corporate bandwidth but also the corporate e-mail resources. Like other forms of hi-jacking malware, spam engines have the potential to generate enormous amounts of traffic from a single device as multiple, simultaneous SMTP connections are attempted. It is not at all unusual for a single spam engine to generate 2 to 3 megabits of sustained traffic flow and consume all system resources.

Porn Dialers

Porn dialers, one of the original forms of malware that generated revenues for bad guys, are still highly profitable and therefore actively propagated. In the case of ICS security they have special significance due to the fact that modem communications are still widely used in

ICS. An ICS device used for either sending SCADA commands or receiving SCADA, PCS, or RTU telemetry on a scheduled basis through a modem would find itself essentially in a denial of service position without a noticeable load on the system. A porn dialer would simply take over the modem and make long calls to toll numbers that end up as charges directly to the organization's phone bill.

A further important consideration related to the large continued presence of dial-up connections in ICS (relative to other industries) is the fact that computers relying on dial-up for network connectivity tend to represent a higher proportion of compromised systems. The reason for this is that many of the patches that must be downloaded are large compared to the download capability on dial-up devices. A modern Microsoft patch bundle is typically between 2 and 10 megabytes in size. This can amount to hours of online time for a dial-up user, and will monopolize the connection for the entire time. Understandably, dial-up users are sometimes reluctant to patch their systems, and therefore the higher incidence of compromise. As a result, remote ICS using commercial operating systems may be unpatched for no other reason than the time it would require to download, say, a 300-megabyte service pack. These machines become especially vulnerable. Even if they are not connecting to the open Internet, they become very soft targets the moment they connect to the corporate network. Pair this with the frequent requirement to not install firewall and antivirus software that is not supported by the ICS vendors and you have a system at risk of rapid and difficult-to-detect malware exploits.

Most worrying of all when it comes to remote systems using a dial-up modem for connection is that if they are compromised by any malware—porn dialer or other—the malware will take control of the modem in its attempts to find a network connection or rack up tolls, making attempts to troubleshoot or regain remote control tougher by virtue of a constant busy signal!

Conclusions on ICS Threats

Much of the threat information available about ICS assets is presented in the same format as threats to IT assets, that is, as information about threat-from—specific information about where the threats are coming from, versus information about the assets actually being targeted. For IT this is mildly actionable given that assets are scattered throughout the infrastructure—basically in every corner of the IT infrastructure, from laptops and USB sticks to data warehouses. In this case, penetration of any variety into the corporate environment is likely to elicit a hit. ICS do not have the same history of ubiquitous access, mobile devices, and heterogeneous user bases behaving in a wide variety of manners. For this reason, threat-from information without threat-to information possesses less actionable value for ICS. Consequently, threat taxonomies that apply to threat agents, means, motivations, and methods are less helpful. In Chapter 4 we will explore the process for obtaining the asset-specific threat-to information that is more meaningful for ICS risk management.

With the advent/discovery of ICS-specific malware as of July 2010, understanding the tradecraft associated with botnet and other forms of hi-jacking malware is important to ICS security practitioners because of the prevalence of these entities within most enterprise networks. Modern malware is conclusively penetrating legacy security controls such as antivirus and intrusion detection systems. Chances are that the random operations of this malware impacting ICS are high, once the corporate network has been infected. This fact, coupled with the increased prevalence of old and unpatched operating systems in ICS networks, makes modern malware a significant threat.

Endnotes

1. http://ThreatChaos.com.
2. http://www.w3schools.com/browsers/browsers_os.asp.
3. http://av-comparatives.org/images/stories/test/ondret/avc_report26.pdf.
4. http://av-comparatives.org.
5. http://www.sans.org.
6. http://www.us.sorbs.net.
7. http://www.spamhaus.org.
8. http://www.sorbs.net.
9. http://ww.spamhaus.org.

3

ICS VULNERABILITIES

In Chapter 2, we discussed the various threats and threat agents aligned against ICS, according to available intelligence, observations, and cited opinions from reputable sources in this field. Vulnerabilities are what threats take advantage of in order to compromise assets, ICS or otherwise. Vulnerabilities affect the likelihood that a threat will be successful in an attack and subsequent attempt to compromise, and vulnerabilities are a major part of the formula behind risk: the nature of the vulnerability influences the likelihood of a threat being successful in exploiting it. The other half of a risk formula is the severity of the resulting impact after the assets have been compromised.

This chapter focuses on ICS vulnerabilities, but not at the granular level of patches, operating systems, protocol flaws, and device-specific fragility. ICS vulnerability is a large problem with many moving parts. Like all large problems, it is best approached first by breaking it down and then attacking the pieces separately rather than as a single, large issue (that would probably never be solved to everyone's satisfaction anyway). This chapter attempts to place ICS vulnerabilities into useful taxonomies in order that they can be categorized, understood, and managed.

We are not going to propose a single methodology of segregating and managing vulnerabilities; rather, we will discuss a variety of approaches, leaving the reader to decide which, if any, can be usefully applied in their own environment. For instance, some taxonomies and methodologies lend themselves most usefully to the development and assessment of technical solutions and architecture design. Others are less technically descriptive but more suitable for processes such as threat risk assessment or supporting management-level reporting and metrics related to ICS vulnerabilities and their impact on productivity or profitability.

The first thing to be addressed is the matter of whether ICS vulnerabilities are distinct from IT vulnerabilities. In Chapter 2 we proposed that the most prominent threats to ICS were largely the same as those to IT, but that they were more likely to successfully degrade or compromise ICS assets as a matter of a random hit as opposed to a directed strike. Such is the prevalence and power of modern malware and its ability to fly through IT and ICS controls alike. However, the matter of vulnerabilities is different. We do not propose that the vulnerabilities of ICS are like those of IT. In fact, we propose they are significantly distinct but not unrecognizable from an IT perspective.

ICS Vulnerability versus IT Vulnerabilities

A major challenge to advancing and developing ICS security controls and safeguards is recognition or acknowledgment by the wider IT security community that while ICS and IT may share many vulnerabilities, the impacts and failure modes of ICS devices are widely different. ICS security practitioners and denizens have a propensity to insist that ICS security is "not the same," but offer few simple and obvious reasons why this is so. In other words, they are failing to express their situation in a concise and easy to appreciate manner. As a result, the (much better defined and documented) world of IT security has often attempted to impose its own standards and methodologies wholesale on the ICS community—only to meet resistance (sometimes warranted, sometimes not). The result has delayed development of ICS security capabilities.

Additionally, IT is frequently characterized by the client-server, where the server is located on a different network and the communications flow from the "edge" of the network to the center, which means it can be more easily monitored, inspected, and de-bugged. See Figure 3.1.

ICS communications frequently involved multiple peer-to-peer and client-server mixes in even a single process instruction, as illustrated in Figure 3.2.

As shown in Figure 3.3, as many as 19 independent layer 2 sessions and 5 TCP (layer 5) sessions may be constructed and destroyed in a single process instruction, most of which are peer to peer. These communications rarely follow the network edge, making the differentiation and inspection of illicit traffic difficult, as it is hard to put the ICS conversation together.

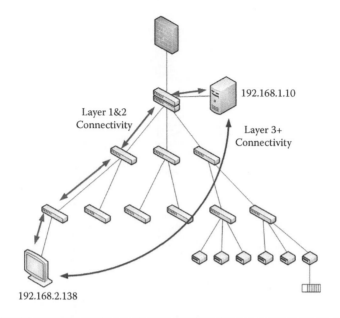

Figure 3.1 IT network flow. (From Singer, Bryan, *Correlating Risk Events and Process Trends to Improve Reliability*, Kenexis, 2010.)

Availability, Integrity, and Confidentiality

Whether ICS or IT, the definitions for *availability*, *integrity*, and *confidentiality* remain the same:

Availability
: Availability is impacted when data cannot be accessed at the time it is needed. Availability impacts may result from accidental or deliberate loss or destruction, or delay in delivery.

Integrity
: Integrity is impacted when data change without authorization. Integrity impacts may result from accidental or deliberate corruption (partial or complete) of data, changing of data. Corruption or change can occur through partial or selective removal/deletion of portions of a data set.

Confidentiality
: Confidentiality is impacted when data are disclosed without authorization. Confidentiality impacts may result from either unapproved or ill-timed disclosure. Disclosure may be to any nonauthorized entities, up to and including the general public.

Figure 3.2 ICS instruction relays among peers. (From Singer, Bryan, *Correlating Risk Events and Process Trends to Improve Reliability*, Kenexis, 2010.)

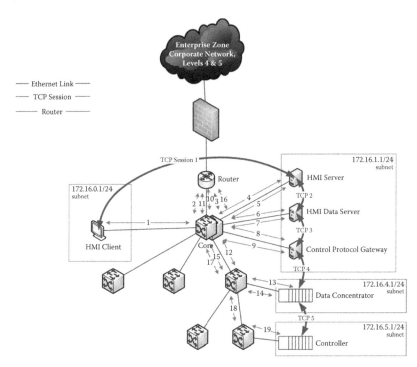

Figure 3.3 ICS control instruction. (From Singer, Bryan, *Correlating Risk Events and Process Trends to Improve Reliability*, Kenexis, 2010.)

In the IT world it is common to discuss the properties of security and assurance in the context of confidentiality, integrity, and availability (CIA), where confidentiality is the property with the most emphasis, integrity next, and availability as the property that would tolerate the least assurance. In many ways this continues to hold true for IT today, where IT is about the management of information in business systems. However, certain classes of IP-based transactions (such as financial transactions in high-frequency trading) that are sometimes considered IT have very high requirements associated with all assurance properties.

Other applications using IP and leveraging, or highly associated with IT applications, are voice-over IP (VOIP) and video of IP, for closed-circuit monitoring and increasingly video on demand or live TV. These applications represent a move away from the traditional hierarchy of CIA, as they place significantly more emphasis on availability and integrity and less on confidentiality.

In the ICS world, the trinity of CIA is less used because it does not reflect the correct order of emphasis. In ICS, availability requires the greatest assurance, followed very closely by integrity (especially if the integrity issues are associated with manipulation of view threats; see Table 3.5). Note that this distinction is only provided as a general guide, as ignoring any aspect of the CIA triad can result in disastrous security failures for ICS. ICS can possess requirements and sensitivities down to the millisecond level, at which point performance degrades and risks increase. Similarly, at that level of availability, complementary issues associated with integrity come into play as the delay and corruption amount to roughly the same thing: loss of view or control, or denial of view or control (more on these impacts shortly).

Confidentiality, as an assurance property, has little to no legacy in ICS systems, which were formerly closed and arcane in operation. In order to gain valuable intelligence for purposes such as espionage, insider-level knowledge or physical access is frequently needed to gain sufficient understanding of the ICS process. The system would have to be tapped and information flows recorded for later reassembly, combined with an insider or insider equivalent understanding of not only the actual process, but also the process type and physics behind the process as well. The difficulty associated with confidentiality attacks, especially in an earlier age of 300-baud (bits per second) networks is the amount of time and the size of the data set required to get a valuable sample size of data. It was far easier to steal production data from files or bribe employees in most cases.

Figure 3.4 qualitatively illustrates the difference between ICS and three other IP-based assets and their assurance requirements associated with the property of availability. ICS is on the far left and availability issues can start at submillisecond interruptions and rapidly escalate to a denial or loss of control situation by the time latency has reached into the range of seconds. Assets such as VOIP or video-over IP (for instance, video conferencing) also become critically impacted at the range of a second delay, but by design can easily tolerate tens of millisecond of delay. In the case of IT (business system communication, messaging, etc.) there is very little noticeable difference in service levels to either the user or the applications until multiple seconds of latency are introduced; meanwhile, the business systems and some entire businesses can function for hours or potentially days without

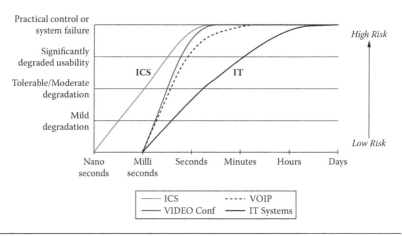

Figure 3.4   Availability requirements for ICS versus other IP-based services.

IT. In effect, the distance between the ICS arch on the left and the IT arch on the right is a graphical representation of how ICS and IT differ according to availability assurance requirements.

Figure 3.5 qualitatively illustrates the difference between ICS and three other IP-based assets and their assurance requirements associated with the property of integrity. ICS is on the far left and integrity issues can start at submillisecond interruptions and rapidly escalate to denial or loss of control situations by the time latency has reached into the range of seconds. Video assets are likely the next most sensitive IP-based system to integrity changes due to the commonality they frequency share with ICS: User Datagram Protocol (UDP).

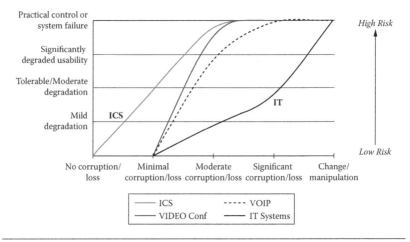

Figure 3.5   Integrity requirements for ICS versus other IP-based services.

UDP is frequently referred to as a connectionless protocol because of its lack of native handshaking and resulting error correction or integrity-checking features. But, UDP is also known for fast delivery of particularly time-sensitive data, such as ICS and video data. VOIP is distinct from ICS and video assets in that it uses the Transmission Control Protocol (TCP), which features handshaking, error correction, and integrity checks. For this reason, VOIP services can accommodate more integrity issues because the underlying protocols will compensate; however, VOIP is also time sensitive and service quality will rapidly degrade with even a moderate level of integrity loss.

IT (business system communication, messaging, etc.), on the other hand, is also based on TCP, but without anything like the time sensitivity (availability) issues of VOIP. IT can tolerate significant integrity issues as long as TCP is compensating; however, as with all systems, IT integrity issues associated with deliberate change or manipulation cannot be addressed by protocols and represent high risks. Once again, the distance between the ICS convex arch on the left and the IT concave arch on the right is a graphical representation of how ICS and IT differ according to integrity assurance requirements.

Figure 3.6 qualitatively illustrates the difference between ICS and three other IP-based assets and their assurance requirements

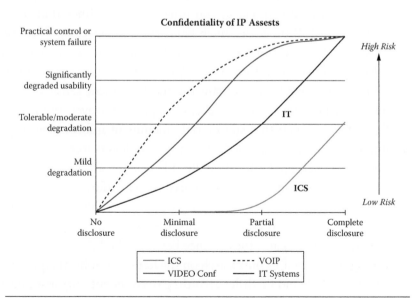

Figure 3.6 Availability requirements for ICS versus other IP-based services.

associated with the property of confidentiality. ICS is on the far right this time, indicating that confidentiality is not a core property of ICS relative to other IP-based assets like IT, voice, and video services. ICS, through a process of both legacy and operational practicality, do not place a premium on confidentiality: most ICS data are about current state and are useful for trending and analysis but not for intelligence associated with assets like plans, strategies, or intellectual property.

As a matter of legacy, ICS evolved on closed proprietary systems where protection against eavesdropping (versus delay/loss/corruption) was considered a low risk.

As a matter of practicality, encryption is a computationally expensive process, increasing the cost and complexity of ICS devices, and thereby their business and operational risks. VOIP may arguably represent the asset most sensitive to any confidentiality breech, starting with mere traffic flow observations which can yield information about who is calling whom, while context might be derived from other sources or inference. Even a small amount of a conversation (keywords, language used, male/female caller), which could be derived from just a handful of successfully captured packets, can represent significant amounts of information to observers. Video streams are less prone but not immune to risks associated with disclosure, because video streams can be associated with both physical security and privacy. Video is also prone to consume at least 4 times (but more typically 50 to 100 times) as much bandwidth as voice, significantly increasing the amount of data that must be successfully intercepted and decrypted to exact information. IT (business system communication, messaging, etc.) may contain the most detailed, sensitive, and context-specific information for eavesdroppers. However, the nature of IT systems is such that substantial amounts of information must be intercepted and reassembled without packet loss before decryption can even be attempted. Additionally, IT systems are very "chatty," and there is a substantial amount of extraneous information relative to actual valuable payload in most IT-based information transactions. For this reason, partial confidentiality breeches may not reveal any information. Once again, the distance between the ICS concave arch on the right and the IT convex arch on the left is a graphical representation of how ICS and IT differ according to confidentiality assurance requirements.

Purdue Enterprise Reference Architecture[1]

One approach to understanding the differences between ICS and IT security requirements is from a granular architecture perspective, using the security properties of confidentiality, integrity, and availability and the Purdue Enterprise Reference Architecture (PERA).

PERA is a useful tool in understanding the distinction between ICS and IT systems because it has been adopted by the ICS community and International Society of Automation (ISA) for representing and designing the interface between ICS and IT. For instance, where ICS and IT systems meet in the business world to share production information with management systems. PERA is a tool that can be used to model and design this interface, though without being specifically intended for this purpose.

PERA recognizes that network architecture must manage assets (programmable logic controllers [PLCs], historians, servers, etc.) at different levels of speed and assurance in order to achieve adequate response, resolution, reliability, and reparability. In PERA, the lowest levels represent the periphery of the network where properties associated with availability are paramount. The higher in the PERA model one moves, the more IT-like assets enter the network and requirements for availability are reduced. By IT-like we mean operating systems and devices that might commonly be found in an IT network but have been implemented to support ICS; for instance, Windows servers or desktop computers that might serve as human–machine interfaces (HMIs).

PERA Levels

Table 3.1 is a snapshot of the PERA levels.

Levels 5 and 4: Enterprise Systems At levels 5 and 4 the primacy of confidentiality versus availability flips, where confidentiality of information becomes more vital than availability.

This level is described as "business planning and logistics" in the ANSI/ISA-95 standards and includes the functions involved in the business-related activities needed to manage a production, transportation, or manufacturing organization.

Table 3.1 PERA Levels

PERA LEVEL	ASSETS	AVAILABILITY REQUIREMENT
Level 5	Production planning, supplier management, product and service strategy, design and development	Days
Level 4	Enterprise resource planning (ERP), finance and accounting systems, HR systems, messaging and productivity tools, production scheduling, maintenance scheduling, manufacturing resource planning, material/product tracking, site-wide production reporting, and inventory management	Hours
Level 3	Area optimization, production data history, maintenance monitoring	Minutes to hours
Level 2	Operator interface, unit optimization, trending (chart recorder replacement), real-time statistical process control	Seconds to minutes
Level 1	Basic control, interlocking	Millisecond to seconds
Level 0	Input/output from sensors actuators	Continuous

Source: PERA FAQ: http://www.pera.net/Pera/faq_Why_Levels.html.

Functions include enterprise or regional financial systems and other enterprise infrastructure components such as production scheduling, operational management, and maintenance management for an individual plant or site in an enterprise.

Level 3: Operations Management   A level 3 system is typically the first level at which traditional multitasking operating system software is available.

Level 3 is also the highest level where the ICS availability requirement dominates over confidentiality requirements typical in IT systems.

Level 3 includes the functions involved in managing the workflows to produce the desired end products. Examples include production management, energy management, system performance monitoring, detailed production scheduling, reliability assurance, on-line process simulation, and site-wide control optimization.

Level 2: Supervisory Control   Level 2 includes the functions involved in monitoring and supervisory control of the physical process.

Level 2 includes the functions to manage specific devices and discrete elements of the workflow. Level 2 functions and equipment include operator human–machine interface (HMI), operator alarms and alerts, supervisory control functions, process history collection, and open loop control[2] with human intervention.

Level 1: Local or Basic Control   Level 1 includes the functions involved in sensing and manipulating the physical process. Process monitoring equipment reads data from sensors, executes algorithms if necessary, and maintains process history. Examples of process monitoring systems include tank gauging systems, continuous emission monitors, rotating equipment monitoring systems, and temperature indicating systems. Process control equipment reads data from sensors, executes a control algorithm, and sends an output to a final element (e.g., control valves or motor controls). Level 1 controllers are directly connected to the sensors and actuators of the process.

Level 1 includes continuous closed-loop control, sequence control, batch control, and discrete control. Many modern controllers include all types of control in a single device.

Also included in level 1 are safety (safety instrumented systems [SIS]) and protection systems that monitor the process and automatically return the process to a safe state if it exceeds safe limits. This category also includes systems that monitor the process and alert an operator of impending unsafe conditions.

Examples of level 1 equipment include distributed control systems (DCS) controllers, SIS controllers, PLCs, and remote terminal unit (RTUs).

Level 0: Process   Level 0 is a purely analogue communication interface referred to as the input/output (I/O), supported by a short run of cable from the infrastructure under management to the control device at level 1. (See the section "Functional Vulnerabilities" later in this chapter, for a detailed discussion of the I/O interface.)

Level 0 is the actual physical process. The process can include any type of production facility in all industrial sectors.

Level 0 includes the sensors and actuators directly connected to the process and process equipment.

Examples of level 0 equipment include transmitters and valve actuators, pumps, temperature sensors, motor controls, and many more infrastructure devices.

Figure 3.7 depicts the PERA model.

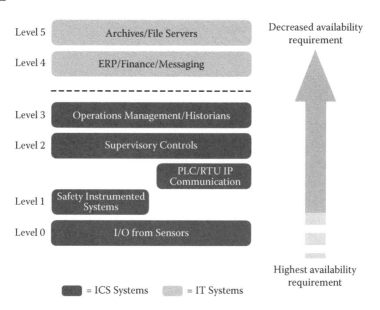

Figure 3.7 PERA reference model.

An Ironic Comment on PERA

PERA was developed by ICS practitioners/academics and uses IT successfully as a contrast and counterpoint to understand ICS; however, PERA actually displays a lack of insight into modern IT that ICS practitioners more frequently accuse their IT peers of possessing! This may be due to the fact that IT has changed substantially in the last few years and PERA appears not to have been updated since approximately 2005. While the PERA model is highly constructive for understanding the distinct granularity and consistent focus on availability issues in ICS security, it should not be considered an absolutely authoritative definition of how ICS is different from IT. It is possible to find hidden but otherwise common IT applications that require level 0 support, and there are many IT IP-based services that operate at level 1.

Other applications other than ICS might be found at PERA level 0. One of the best examples of another application running at level 0 is modern financial trading and transaction systems. In this age of high-frequency trading[3] (HFT) these transitions are occurring at microsecond (millionths of a second) timings and fortunes are being made and lost on this basis. The speed and availability requirements for HFT are such that traders and brokerage houses are striving to physically locate their servers as close to exchanges as possible to literally save the distance that light must travel through fiber optics. The distances of fiber runs are considered significant plus or minus 1,000 feet. Given that light travels at roughly 1 foot per nanosecond, this amounts to tuning financial system networks and assurance properties to the microsecond (millionth of a second) level: a degree of sensitivity that even ICS networks are not widely considered to possess. And what happens when the availability of these HFT systems degrades? One possible example is the sudden, dramatic drop of financial markets on May 6, 2010, when the Dow Jones dropped by over 1,000 points (10%) in 5 minutes and then rebounded. The final reason for the plunge has not been determined, but HFT systems running amok is high on the list of culprits,[4] and a temporary breakdown in HFT network speeds among the contributing factors: a bulge may have built up as network latency climbed above millisecond (thousands of seconds) speeds in New York, and when they picked up again (to a "normal" <200 microsecond rate) the sudden rash of backlogged orders resulted in a crazy swing.

At PERA level 1 a wide variety of converged applications based entirely on IP protocols can be found: VOIP and video conferencing are two easy examples. Both of these systems become rapidly unusable once latency (speed) passes about 60 milliseconds. Similarly, as more and more people are using IP-based services for their critical infrastructure such as home phones, the lowly domestic Internet infrastructure starts to acquire level 1 type availability requirements. Could it be that our home networks are in fact the ICS of the future?

Data at Rest, Data in Use, Data in Motion

Data are frequently considered to exist in three states: at rest, in use, and in motion, as illustrated in Figure 3.8. These three states provide another useful paradigm for understanding the distinctions between ICS and IT systems, and therefore the distinct vulnerabilities faced by these systems.

Data in motion is data moving through a network. These data have been segmented into packets, and each packet may take a different route to the destination. Data in motion either may be encrypted using session encryption techniques like secure socket layer (SSL) or have

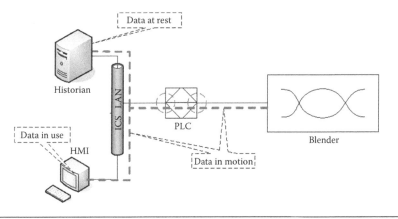

Figure 3.8 Data in motion, at rest, and in use.

been encrypted with a static technique such as an asymmetric, public key system before being segmented into packets. To change or compromise data in motion in an ICS or other system could be as simple as injecting erroneous packets (an integrity attack), or would require that it is intercepted and transformed into data at rest, changed, and then sent back out into a state of motion toward its intended destination. This is typically referred to as a man-in-the-middle (MITM) attack.

Data at rest are retained within the memory of a device or storage system. This memory is nonvolatile and will be retained even if the device is turned off. For instance, data at rest can be contained within databases, on hard disks, or in flat files in local memory or within USB sticks.

Data in use are present within the volatile memory of information processing devices or displayed on the screens of man–machine interface devices (like a PC display or HMI). Data in use will disappear if the device that is using it is turned off. Data in use within ICS devices have little scope for manipulation or change because the devices themselves do not possess the memory or processing power that would allow data in use to be changed deliberately.

ICS, due to its nature of supporting live operations, places a priority on data in motion that must be protected because of the availability requirements. It is also the case that ICS data often have diminished or possibly very little value once they are actually stored/placed at rest. Data at rest for ICS often lose value rapidly as they age and recede from the point in time where they were created and reflected the current state of the production process under control. Historical data stores of a few seconds or minutes are certainly critical to understand trends in processes, but as the age approaches hours, the value to actual production control decreases. (However, the value of this historical data to IT systems like enterprise resource planning may be maintained far longer, but at this point the data asset has migrated from an ICS asset to an IT asset and therefore an IT-security domain.)

Conversely, with IT systems, threats to data at rest are often considered the most numerous, possibly because security controls on data in motion in the IT work are well defined and hardened by this time through transmission encryption techniques. For many IT applications the threat to data in motion lies in the interception and reconstitution of these data—a confidentiality threat.

Distinguishing Business, Operational, and Technical Features of ICS

Security controls have been categorized as being business (management), operational, or technical in nature.[5] This categorization was developed initially for IT systems but can be applied to ICS usefully and without loss of either comprehension or pride.

A business control deals with standards compliance and regulatory issues, contracted covenants, service levels, or other management drivers like business strategies. A business control would generally be expressed as a policy, which would drive and guide the implementation of appropriate operational procedures and technical controls to meet top-level management issues that might not be otherwise obvious on the ground. For instance, a business control may be that the ICS must be ISA-99 compliant according to a qualified third-party opinion. Management may establish this policy in order to show due care and avoid liability under the Environmental Protection Act or other regulatory requirements.

An operational control deals with procedures for operators, technicians, and staff who must perform duties in consistent manners to meet standards or remain compliant with policy. An operational control could consist of generalized guidelines to assure quality and timeliness, and reduce variability, defects, flaws, errors, and omissions. An operational control could also consist of detailed step-by-step instructions and very specific metrics around what constitutes acceptable outputs, whether they be goods or services. Operational controls should implement the policy established by business or management controls and would be created by either operational teams or subject matter experts for use by operational teams.

A technical control deals with hardware and software-based security safeguards. These devices and applications will be managed using the operational controls, which are in turn designed to map to the top-level management controls. A technical control could consist of a firewall, intrusion detection application within the network, antivirus software on a server, or many other elements. Technical controls can be active, whereby they stop malicious activity once it is detected, or passive, where they alert on suspicious activity but do not interrupt operational data flows or application processing. Generally, a technical control can be configured to support a wide range of functions and operational requirements, but should be implemented, tested, and audited against the specific operational and management controls and requirements.

Table 3.2 through Table 3.4 consider the differences between IT and ICS from the perspective of typical management, operational, and

Table 3.2   Business Controls: ICS Distinguishing Features

DISTINCT BUSINESS CONTROL POSTURE IN ICS	
1.	Regulated industries where tariffs are approved by public sector enforcement agencies	Large ICS user industries such as energy, transportation, and water might be regulated to point of having pricing of goods and services preapproved by authorities. This means that ICS investment business plans, amortized over 15 or 20 years, often cannot be adjusted without applying for tariff increases. The result is a massive political effort fraught with a wide variety of other risks related to public relations and other unpredictable issues around regulatory compliance. ICS security cannot necessarily be implemented or redesigned without significant costs that must be absorbed from existing budgets, because regulatory approval for fee hikes will take a long time if it is even possible.
2.	Cost of capital issues are closer to the surface with ICS security	Cost of capital is related to the price paid in interest on debt (bonds) or the value of traded shares (stocks). For large ICS users, security failures in ICS can have major, externally obvious impacts. A major product recall or environmental disaster brought about by flaws in ICS security will have immediate impacts on the equity value of publicly traded entities, and raise borrowing costs of even publicly owned ICS user entities. Additionally, ratings agencies such as Standard & Poors are considering operational risk management when rating equity and debt risks for investors; thus the ability of poor ICS security decisions to drive of cost of capital increases.

Table 3.3 Operational Controls: ICS Distinguishing Features

DISTINCT OPERATIONAL CONTROL POSTURE IN ICS		
1.	Uncommon to have ICS staff dedicated to security	With IT systems it is typical to have staff specifically trained and dedicated to the security and assurance of the IT servers and assets. In most ICS, operational staff are left to also cope with security, without the benefit of specific training or budgets. This lack of specialization means that a variety of checks and balances that typically exist for IT are unavailable for ICS. For instance, system administrators might also be security testers on the same systems, and have access to all elements of the systems, including audit logs. Alternately, no audit functions exist, and therefore oversight of inappropriate security practices is not observed, let alone reported and acted upon.
2.	No development and test environments requires flawless planning	Many ICS were not originally developed with system security in mind, and methodologies related to readiness and testing were not anticipated. The deployment of upgrade patches or other security elements such as firewalls or IDS services cannot be tested in development environments, because they may not exist for reasons associated with cost or the difficulty of accurately simulating an operational environment in a lab. Therefore the design of security controls for existing, legacy ICS must be undertaken with a deep understanding of the systems, because they may be deployed directly to an operational environment. Alternately, plant maintenance cycles must be observed and any ICS deployments must occur at specific times, complete on time, and the next opportunity in the event of a mistake may be months or more away.
3.	IT-like security is not part of life cycle cost calculations	ICS have very long life cycles (as high as 20 to 30 years)—four to five times longer than IT cycles. It is frequently the case that security has not been included into the original amortization, maintenance calculations, and business cases, and is therefore unaffordable. If not unaffordable, then entire financial plans will need to be recalculated and justifications submitted to management and possibly regulators, accompanied by potentially humiliating explanations about why the security requirements were not adequately addressed originally.
4.	Assumptions associated with security design are not the same	ICS vulnerabilities are very likely grossly underreported (see the section "Technical Vulnerabilities" later in this chapter), and therefore management of these systems must account for substantially more unknown risks than IT. Assumptions that are commonplace in IT security design do not apply; for instance, that all devices on the network can tolerate broadcast traffic is a typical IT assumption. Another IT assumption is that malicious activity on the network is essentially transparent to all systems except those compromised or under direct attack. Other previously mentioned assumptions include that systems can be taken offline for patching and tweaking if they are not deployed correctly the first time, and that endpoint devices can generally be enhanced or loaded with additional routines or software as required to address new and emerging security issues. Such assumptions do not play out in ICS.

Table 3.4 Technical Controls: ICS Distinguishing Features

DISTINCT TECHNICAL CONTROL REQUIREMENTS IN ICS	
1. Legacy systems exceedingly difficult to patch or upgrade	The integrated and embedded systems on ICS endpoint devices such as PLCs and RTUs were not designed with extra memory or storage to accommodate new software; in fact, they are often not intended to be upgraded at all. Flaws contained within the software running these devices, whether the protocol stack or the process control routines, must be accommodated until the device is removed from service. Similarly, ICS infrastructures such as data historians or HMI consoles are often based upon highly vulnerable, end of life operating systems such as Windows 98 or NT. Vendors frequently do not support MS patches and do not provide upgrades for their own software to support OS patching.
2. Dispersed assets with mandatory requirement for remote access	Many ICS will have endpoint devices located in remote locations, sometimes at extreme distances from populated areas. In these circumstances operators use any and every possible means of establishing remote command and control connects, because the options are frequently limited, for instance, analogue modems, packet radio, WiMAX, cellular, satellite, etc. This means that ICS security administrators may have to manage an assortment of inbound connections through firewalls, coming over and through networks that are not only untrusted, but possibly run by unknown entities. (Consider an American multination oil firm operating an oil pipeline in the Niger Delta, or a Canadian mining company operating an gold ore extract and processing facility in New Guinea.) Similarly, the ICS culture is one of tight integration between ICS vendors and owners. Unlike the IT world, ICS users will very frequently outsource large portions on their infrastructure to the manufacturers of the different components. These vendors will also require remote access to not only remote devices but also centralized devices (since they are not located on-site and need emergency support access).
3. Safety is not designed into IT security vendor products, where kinetic impacts resulting from control failures are unknown	IT system breaches can result in massive losses in terms of privacy, intellectual property, fraud, compliance, reputation, and goodwill. But ICS breaches can literally injure/kill people and can destroy millions of dollars in property and result in billions of dollars in liability. The notion of "failing safe" is not part of the typical design requirement of IT devices.

technical security. These tables highlight issues that are especially common, and especially different, depending on whether IT or ICS is the target infrastructure.

ICS Vulnerabilities

We spent the first part of this book discussing how ICS is different from IT, in order to better express how ICS vulnerabilities are distinct from IT vulnerabilities: one discussion cannot effectively occur without the other. Too often it is the case that ICS practitioners do not adequately or convincingly express the differences between ICS and IT, and as a result their claims of unique vulnerabilities and the requirement for unique risk treatment are unattended.

Vulnerabilities unique to ICS are poorly understood, especially when compared to the massive body of work and research around IT vulnerabilities and threats. In this section we will address some fundamental approaches to organizing and categorizing ICS vulnerabilities and threats in manners necessarily unique from existing IT approaches.

As previously discussed, information and communication management systems, whether ICS or IT, can express their controls and therefore associated vulnerabilities in the same three classes: management, operations, and technical.

Management Vulnerabilities

In the context of management (policy and governance) controls, the following vulnerabilities are identified as common within ICS user organizations:

- *Enterprise risk management (ERM)*—ERM practices, exercises, and documentation are not typical in all types of business, including among ICS users. An ERM exercise should document the top of mind strategic risks that executive management considers "make or break" for the business. A common lack of an ERM exercise makes it difficult for ICS managers to link the security of ICS to high-level corporate goals: without this linkage available in the clear(er) requirements and guidance contained in an ERM, resources will remain difficult to obtain for ICS controls.
- *Policies identifying roles and accountability*—When it is security policy these are inadequate, an indication of a lack of management-level profile or priority. Directly related are governance and oversight, which should officially engage top management in the ICS security issues to raise awareness. This is not to imply that management should be involved in engineering decisions or incident management; more likely they would have visibility through scheduled

reports around issues such as ICS incidents and outages that might be related to security. As a result of inadequate policies and governance, ownership for ICS security is often poorly defined, and therefore responsibility is not assigned. Without responsibility there is not accountability in the upper echelons of ICS user organizations.

- *Ad hoc budgets and one-time (or nonexistent) investment*— ICS security is a program, not a point in time exercise. Similarly, ICS security budgets benefit substantially from being clearly defined line items in management budgets that appear year after year. Too often ICS security is funded from discretionary budgets, which can shift or even disappear from year to year. The resulting funding base is unstable and ICS security programs cannot prosper or mature in such an environment.

- *Lack of management engagement*—Finally, even without official policy, governance, or doctrine related to ICS security, there still remains the issue of guidance of any sort—even if it comes without resources or official support. Lack of guidance requires the "least effort" to address, because it can consist of simply directives such as "refer to NIST 800-82." Guidance can also be related to simple high-level concepts such as the use of defense in depth strategies, identifying management and access control requirements, and the use of cryptography, yet this guidance is typically lacking.[6] Ideally, management would provide detailed guidance such as an ERM report, as discussed above, spelling out the compliance issues and standards that must be addressed.

Operational Vulnerabilities

In the context of operational (procedural) controls, the following vulnerabilities are identified as common within ICS user organizations:

- *Segregating ICS traffic from business data traffic*—Often, ICS networks will be extended into business network zones to bring production data to business systems such as enterprise resource planning (ERP) applications. In the course of extending the networks, the ICS network is simply overlaid on the IT business network with minimum or sometimes no separation at all: not even logical separation with different subnets. While physically distinct networks for ICS and IT are not generally practical or desirable, a variety of logical segregation techniques can be applied. The danger with weak or no segregation is that malware and malicious entities in the relatively open IT business network "hop" unopposed into the ICS network.

- *Separation of duties for administrative accounts and roles—* Within the ICS network, administrative efficiency often encourages poor security practices, such as sharing administrator accounts, complete overlap of administrative duties, and common passwords. In the event of an incident (accidental or malicious), it becomes nearly impossible to attribute accountability or even perform forensics. In the event of a malicious outsider or insider gaining access to an overprivileged account, he or she can delete logs, set file permissions, and generally tamper with systems in an untraceable manner. (Note: This is a top vulnerability in IT systems too.)

- *Remote access procedures to support audit, multilevel access, and forensics—*Allowing third-party suppliers into the ICS network is a common and often mandatory requirement for support and maintenance purposes. Controlling this access, the accounts engendered and the "privilege creep" associated with the remote access accounts are frequent weak points in ICS. Not just ICS, but IT systems too face massive problems in this area, and spawned a specific discipline: identity and access management (IAM). IAM challenges are not limited to remote access accounts but because of the increased use of the Internet and the ubiquitous use of old-fashioned modem pools connected to the public switched telephone network (PSTN), attribution, audit, and governance associated with remote support and management on ICS are critical.

- *Wireless systems deployment and hardening guidelines—*If design and architecture are a problem within the physical sites between the ICS and IT business networks, then the problem can be expected to crop up in the increasing use of wireless technologies. Compounding the problem is that many wireless connections are being deployed for remote ICS devices, trunking, and back-haul from site to site using off-the-shelf, fully interoperable equipment with standards such as IEEE 802.11b/g/n or WiMax (IEEE 802.16) or mildly tweaked variants. These networks are exceedingly easy to detect and, with poor design and architecture added into the mix, can be highly susceptible to eavesdropping and masquerade attacks by the curious and saboteurs alike.

- *Internet as a communications channel without hardening guidelines*—Like wireless systems, the Internet is an offer too good to refuse for linking up remote devices and offices with central ICS servers. It is far cheaper to buy a dial-up modem account from a local ISP or data services from the local cellular firm (so it appears "wireless" again) than it is to install leased phone lines with permanent connections made to the ICS network, or even to make long-distance calls from a remote modem to the dial-in pool. The vulnerabilities come into play not with these access approaches for ICS devices, but in the ad hoc deployment and configuration of the access architectures and devices. Poorly hardened systems on the Internet are compromised in a matter of minutes; yet administrators operating without proper operational procedures and guidelines, or a decent policy framework, will inevitably deploy vulnerable systems.

- *Incident detection, response, and reporting procedures*—As often as not, a specific procedure to detect an incident is not required: you know when something is wrong with the system. In fact, that is one of the core functions of the ICS in the first place. But not always. Sometimes, compromises can be difficult to diagnose and triage, and procedures to employ consistent evaluation techniques can be invaluable when dealing with marginal indicators. Given that the best malware is designed to stay below the radar, it is all about understanding the marginal symptoms. Response processes are an area of poor focus in many ICS operational programs, at least when it comes to ICT threats (versus too much pressure or heat). Response processes make the difference between a coordinated, efficient, and effective approach to a potentially serious threat and emerging hazard, and a botched job and its associated consequences. This situation is by no means unique to ICS and is a common shortcoming of IT business systems too, but as we have been saying, ICS is different. Finally, the adage "you cannot manage what you cannot measure" comes into play when reporting ICS security incidents. Too often ICS operators will deal with risk events, yet fail to formally record the metrics associated with the event. How was the product impacted, by quantifiable losses in availability, productivity, or defects? Data lost? How much? Hours spent during recovery? How many? Dollars spent on overtime and contractors? How much? Without incident reporting procedures to apply consistency, justifying investment in security is tough. What else is tough is learning from mistakes, because the fine details of a software or network in crisis tend to disappear from memory once the event passes and you get the system back up again!

- *Change management controls on all IT and ICS assets in the ICS network*—The ability to manage system upgrades, patches, reconfiguration of servers or networks, virtualization (moving from dedicated to virtualized and cluster platforms), and most other changes to the logical environment can be a problem for any organization, ICS or otherwise. ICS environments, because of their fragility, tend to have better change management than the typical IT environment, but lapses in operational practices are still common. Poor change management represents a huge risk because it can induce both immediate failures and established "time bombs" that do not become apparent until a specific and discrete set of activities occur to generate an unanticipated hazard, probably at a time when response capabilities are not at their maximum, such as after hours. Poor change management within adjacent IT systems is another vulnerability for ICS, where a failure on the IT side cascades into the ICS side. For instance, routers and switches may be shared network assets, or they may be dedicated to ICS but managed by the IT group due to the scare skills required to configure and manage enterprise networks. A change management weakness in IT may result in a catastrophic network failure across the organization, impacting both IT and ICS since the assets under management (routers and switches) supported both network types. The lack of acceptance testing environments can also accentuate the change management issue in ICS.

• *Acceptance testing and vulnerability testing procedures of IT and ICS assets on the ICS network*—Acceptance testing involves putting new, upgraded, patched, or otherwise changed assets through predetermined tests to see if they perform as expected. An important part of acceptance testing, but frequently overlooked, is vulnerabilities testing. Vulnerabilities testing should be part of the overall test plan, and should check that the upgrades, patches, reconfigurations, and so forth, did not introduce new vulnerabilities. For instance, an upgrade to an application—say a historian—may result in new ports being opened up on the server, such as directory or database management ports. These services may not be hardened as part of the application configuration and subject to simple, known attacks. The fact that the ICS network supports the application is no excuse for leaving these ports untreated; as we have already discussed, the ways and means for modern malware to gain access to ICS networks are ever growing. Modern malware, in its search to exploit new devices and recruit them for illicit purposes, may take advantage of new services introduced by asset changes that cannot be addressed through acceptance testing. Acceptance testing, if done properly, requires a simulated operating environment and data flows, or a specially set-aside testing environment in order to be properly conducted. In the case of ICS, this can be especially challenging for two primary reasons: (1) The cost of simulating an ICS environment in a meaningful fashion can be higher than for an IT environment, and therefore is a cost that is forgone. In an IT environment, systems are these days established on virtual operating systems and platforms that can be built, destroyed, and rebuilt in a matter of seconds. Many simulation and testing tools exist for IT in order to generate traffic and data flows to systems so that testing is as close to reflecting the operating conditions as possible. Even assets such as telephones, video cameras, or other physically grounded endpoints can be readily replicated in software with off-the-shelf tools. ICS simulation tools are not as readily available, potentially requiring the very costly development of mock infrastructure, including control rooms and real endpoint devices (PLCs/RTUs) in order to simulate an operational environment. (2) For older ICS infrastructure using equipment 15 years old but with 10 years of amortization remaining, spares for testing may have never been purchased or budgeted, and may no longer be available from manufacturers.

Technical Vulnerabilities

Much of the focus on ICS vulnerabilities is often placed upon technical vulnerabilities, that is, vulnerabilities that have their place in hardware, software, or networks. There are long lists of these vulnerabilities available from a number of sources, but the truth is that any list is probably incomplete. Incomplete because the rate of vulnerability discovery in software is formidable, and because the state of research in ICS vulnerabilities is still moderate. For instance, the Common Vulnerabilities and Exposures (CVE) database, hosted by Mitre Corporation for the Department of Homeland Security (DHS), contains 46,490 vulnerabilities at the time of this writing, of which 45 appear to be ICS related.[7] This represents about 0.1% of the total formally reported vulnerabilities. It has been reported that Idaho National Laboratory (INL), over the course of 5 years of ICS security research, has a (nonpublic) catalogue of approximately 325 ICS vulnerabilities,[8] while a Canadian ICS security firm called Wurldtech claims to have a database of over 500 ICS-specific vulnerabilities[9]; assuming the highest claim (500), the potential population of ICS vulnerabilities is up to 1.1% when combined with IT CVEs. By comparison, ICS industry experts suggest that a reasonable representation in CVE would be about 10%[10] given the number of ICS devices deployed in the field and the range of vendors/manufacturers. In other words, common ICS vulnerabilities may be underrepresented in CVE by up to 89.9%. The necessary conclusion, even compensating for a large overestimation of a "reasonable representation" of ICS devices, is that a disproportional number of undocumented ICS vulnerabilities persist. A related conclusion is that assessing risk to ICS based entirely or even partially upon known vulnerabilities is questionable.

For these reasons, our discussion on technical ICS vulnerabilities will seek to establish useful frameworks for assessing and describing vulnerabilities, rather than specific vulnerabilities themselves. The benefit of this approach is that vulnerabilities that are unique to ICS become easier to recognize once a descriptive paradigm has been established. By understanding in a generic manner how to describe and where to expect vulnerabilities in any ICS, it becomes easier to describe them in our own systems. From here, the ability to effectively describe and recognize vulnerabilities (or potential vulnerabilities) makes it easier to gather the appropriate metrics to support business cases for remediation and investment.

Functional of Vulnerabilities

A useful approach to understanding and identifying ICS vulnerability is to create a taxonomy that reflects functional properties as opposed to attempting to categorize and group vulnerabilities through attack modes like denial of service or privilege escalation. Given that a major operation vulnerability of ICS is the lack of testing and redundant environments, and the kinetic nature of impacts, waiting around for patterns of impact to appear and noting them is not an option.

Viewing an ICS control device as two distinct communications interfaces is an important first part of a vulnerability taxonomy based on assurance, as illustrated in Figure 3.9. One interface is the IP communications interface on the IP network, to which an operator issues commands from an HMI or SCADA server. This is also the interface that would be subject to attack and presents the interface that a cyber threat may exploit remotely as well as locally. The other communications interface is the input/output (I/O) control interface, where the physical functions of the production infrastructure are controlled through analogue communication, typically over short distances (<10 meters). The I/O interface is physically connected to valves, sensors, drives, and so forth, and controls the physical behaviors of the system. Figure 3.6 illustrates the distinction between the two interfaces to be found on an ICS control device. Not shown in Figure 3.6 is the extent

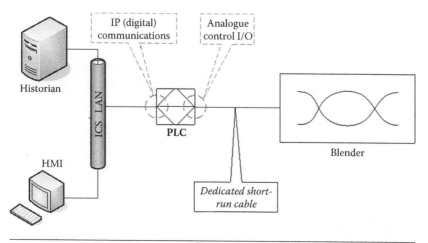

Figure 3.9 Digital and analogue interfaces.

to which the ICS network is interconnecting with other networks, including internal business networks and the "foreign" networks of suppliers, partners, and clients.

It is useful to understand the two different interfaces, because they can be related to different forms of vulnerability: degradation of communications or degradation of I/O control, where communications equates with "view." Many of the vulnerabilities discovered to date exhibit different behaviors impacting primarily the communications interface; however, some of the vulnerabilities have also been shown to result in dangerous failures when the functioning of the analogue I/O is disabled or modified in an indeterminate way, resulting in erratic behavior potentially resulting in kinetic (physical) impacts.

ICS controls devices such as PLCs and RTUs are relatively simple with little latitude for sophisticated exploits. There are no escalation of privilege attacks because there is usually only one level of privilege: administrator. If you can logically reach an ICS device, your alternatives for vulnerability exploitation fall neatly but broadly into six alternative classes with identifiable but not absolute functional impacts: denial of view, loss of view, manipulation of view, and denial of control, loss of control, and manipulation of control. This is illustrated in Table 3.5.

Depending on the state of the ICS network under consideration, some or even all the six classes of functional vulnerability may be present. From the perspective of risk management and reporting, this

Table 3.5 Class of ICS Vulnerability

	DENIAL (TEMPORARY)	LOSS (SUSTAINED)	MANIPULATION
View	DoV	LoV	MoV
Control	DoC	LoC	MoV
WHITE	View is disrupted but not control. Disruption to reporting and operator awareness. Production and infrastructure risks primarily if the condition remains undetected or goes unaddressed for long periods of time.		
GRAY	Control is disrupted. Impacts (temporary or sustained) on communication interface can result in an erratic or "frozen" condition on the IP communications interface, but leaves the control interface otherwise stable and the logic intact. Risk varies widely with the process under control.		
BLACK	View and/or control cannot be recovered automatically or remotely. Sabotage potential through misinformation delivered to control room personnel, or through malicious instructions sent to production infrastructure. Risk is highest.		

taxonomy allows for a rapid triage type assessment and reporting to management. An advantage of using an abbreviated reporting taxonomy is that technical details can be saved for technical appendixes, and the most salient information reported to management using a simple scale that can be summarized in a single slide.

> *Denial of view (DoV)*—Results from a temporary IP communication interface failure, where the interface recovers and becomes available once the interfering condition abates. Under this condition, the control logic within the PLC/RTU may continue to function even if a DoV occurs. Loss of production information can appear as a slowdown in production and generate cascading (and unwarranted) slowdowns in other parts of the production process while the interference persists. Enterprise reporting systems can also be impacted, providing inaccurate guidance to management while the interference persists. Denial of accurate view of production infrastructure also creates the risk of operators taking inappropriate or harmful actions due to the inaccurate knowledge of the system state.
>
> *Loss of view (LoV)*—Results from a sustained or permanent IP communication interface failure where the device will require local, hands-on operator intervention, for instance,

a restart. Under this condition, the control logic within the PLC/RTU can continue to function even if a LoV occurs. Loss of production information can appear as a slowdown in production and generate cascading (and unwarranted) slow-downs in other parts of the production process until a local operator can restore functionality. Enterprise reporting systems can also be impacted, providing inaccurate guidance to management until a local operator can restore functionality. Loss of accurate view of production infrastructure also creates the risk of operators taking inappropriate or harmful actions due to the inaccurate knowledge of the system state.

Manipulation of view (MoV)—Harmful actions are possible in scenarios where misinformation (forged ICS data) is used to encourage inappropriate operator responses. MoV does not impact the functionality of the IP communications interface or the I/O control interface. MoV can dupe operators into inappropriate control sequences that introduce defects and possibly catastrophic reactions within the production process. Enterprise reporting systems can also be contaminated with erroneous information providing inaccurate guidance to management. MoV in an ICS infrastructure creates the risk of operators taking inappropriate or harmful actions due to the deliberately falsified information about the system state. Alternately, it could happen that a DoV situation generates errors that simulate legitimate ICS data to the HMI/historian, and equate to an MoV. In this instance, a fault is tripped in an ICS device that results in the device continuing to send false "status OK" variant messages back to the SCADA/DCS even while a process failure escalates.

Denial of control (DoC)—A temporary inability to control resulting from either energized or de-energized I/O interface. DoC can be unintentional or intentional: unintentional DoC includes operator accidents, hardware failures, or DOV conditions that have a negative, systemic impact on the I/O interface, such as network failures or improper network capacity. For instance, it is possible that an attack on an ICS device such as a PLC is directed specifically at flaws in the IP communications stack; however, the systemic interactions on the device between the IP communications stack and the analogue I/O interface cause the I/O interface to fail or stop behaving according to its programming. Once the degradation or interference on the IP communications interface clears and the communications interface returns to normal, the I/O control interface resumes its programmed behaviors. Intentional DoC can result from a threat against the I/O control interface which does not impact the IP communications interface, but disables the I/O control interface, possibly allowing operators to actually see how the ICS device engages in erratic or unprogrammed behavior without any ability to control it. In DoC situations, control of the I/O interface is restored once the threat has been removed.

Loss of control (LoC)—A sustained loss or race/runaway conditions in which operators cannot issue any commands even if the threat has receded. LoC can be unintentional or intentional: like DoC, unintentional LoC includes operator accidents, hardware failures, or temporary DOV conditions that have a sustained, systemic impact on the I/O interface. For instance, it is possible that an attack on an ICS device such as a PLC is directed specifically at flaws in the IP communications stack; however, the systemic interactions on the device between the IP communications interface and the analogue I/O interface cause the I/O interface to permanently fail or stop behaving according to its programming. Intentional LoC can result from a threat against the I/O control interface that does not impact the IP communications stack, but disables the I/O control interface, possibly allowing operators to actually see how the ICS device engages in erratic or unprogrammed behavior without any ability to control it. In LoC situations, control of the I/O interface can only be restored by local operator intervention, such as a device restart.

Manipulation of control (MoC)—Under this condition, the control logic within the PLC/RTU can be reprogrammed by a third party, and legitimate operator commands overridden. MoC does not impact the functionality of the IP communications interface or the I/O control interface. MoC can override or intercept and change operator commands and apply inappropriate control sequences that introduce defects and possibly catastrophic reactions within the production process. MoC in an ICS infrastructure creates the risk of malicious third parties assuming control of the production infrastructure and deliberately invoking critical errors to ruin production or destroy infrastructure—as was demonstrated by the U.S. Department of Defense (DoD) in the Aurora experiments, where a power generator was issued an ICS command set resulting in its self-destruction.[11]

The functional vulnerabilities described above are useful in analyzing previously known failures or unknown ICS vulnerabilities. For example, by reviewing LoV or MoV opportunities in a system, security analysts and control engineers can assess the potential for an inaccurate or manipulated view of the current system state, which could lead operators to take potentially harmful actions. An example of such a practice is the follow-on actions associated with the 2005 BP Texas City refinery explosion in which there were a number of operator actions taken that exacerbated the catastrophic failure— actions that were based on loss of view. A full case history is available from the U.S. Chemical Safety Board (CSB),[12] and an excellent video from CSB is available on YouTube.[13] It is important to note that the Texas City incident was not intentional, but has been used as a basic study by many security professionals as an example of how a targeted security attack could be launched. This basic analysis associated with broad functional vulnerabilities has been used in the development of a variety of threat models and attack scenarios against oil and gas, power, water, and critical manufacturing processes.

ICS Technical Vulnerability Class Breakdown

With the proposed taxonomy of ICS vulnerability classes, it is good to understand how and where vulnerabilities are actually represented within these classes. If it turns out that some of the classes cannot be associated with any previously detected ICS vulnerabilities, then perhaps they in fact do not exist except in theory. Figure 3.10 shows how the different classes as observed through documented

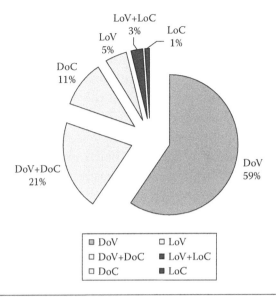

Figure 3.10 ICS vulnerability class breakdown.

vulnerabilities inducing impacts in ICS devices, excluding manipulation. These findings relate to the 500+ ICS vulnerabilities contained in the (closed source/nonpublic) Delphi database from Wurldtech Security Technology.

The largest class of ICS vulnerabilities by far is related to denial of view (DoV), which indicates that the most common vulnerability does not impact I/O control with systemic impacts or erratic behaviors, and view will rapidly return once the exploitation ceases (see Figure 3.8). However, the next largest proportion (21%) shows an impact associated with DoV and denial of control (DoC) combined, where erratic behavior or failure was detected in the I/O control interface while the exploitation continued, but control returned shortly after the exploitation ceased. While loss of view (LoV) represents sustained conditions requiring local intervention or reset of the IP communications interface, the I/O control logic is not impacted. This impact of LoV varies widely from process to process, in general the resulting risk is relatively manageable compared to loss of control (LoC) vulnerabilities. In total, 4% of vulnerabilities lead to LoC conditions in which the I/O control behavior is erratic or the interface becomes de-energized and completely nonresponsive. These are serious failures because of the unpredictability of the resulting risks and the possible need to impact actual production in order to recover/reset the ICS device.

Vulnerability reports specifically associated with manipulation of view (MoV) and manipulation of control (MoC) do not exist. So why do we include them in the taxonomy, if lack of evidence means they could be little more than theory? MoV is considered to be a serious vulnerability associated with a motivated and skilled threat-agent, MoV also requires a substantial amount of system knowledge. For instance, the attackers would need to understand not only the communications protocols and data heuristics of the system under attack, but also the minute details of the control room and operational procedures. This knowledge would be required in order to anticipate responses and illicit a desired sequence of commands that might result in damage to products or production infrastructure. Similarly, the MoV attacker will have to anticipate secondary sources of information that might be used as safeguard/correlating metrics for ensuring that ICS instructions are valid. This could include separate data from other ICS elements within the infrastructure.

Among ICS security practitioners, MoV is considered a substantial potentiality and therefore vulnerability. The previously cited Aurora generator experience[14] was an example of an MoC attack. MoC has also been cited as the potential reason for the wide-scale blackouts in Spain in 2007.[15] While MoC is definitely the bogey man of ICS security, there are few acknowledged incidents to cite and little to no forensic information available. However, given that ICS devices and networks typically contain few security capabilities themselves, MoC would become a relatively simple matter on a more sophisticated IT platform (like a Windows device) once the ICS network was compromised and used as a vector for attack.

Technical Vectors of Attack

In our discussion of technical vulnerabilities of ICS we have so far covered classes of vulnerability and how these classes are useful for building test plans and business cases, gathering metrics, and generally expressing vulnerability issues at a high level to management.

Once again we are going to refrain from attempting to enumerate specific technical vulnerabilities, if for no other reason than that such an effort would probably be out of date before this book went to press. Not only that, but the field of ICS research is revealing new vulnerability information all the time, and we fundamentally do not know what we do not know. However, like the classes of ICS vulnerability, there are also several attack vectors that appear repeatedly not only in formally documented vulnerability reports, but also in anecdotes and the popular press. Understanding attack vectors is useful at a generic level because it allows the ICS operator to review his or her own system with a framework for detecting specific and systemic vulnerabilities.

IT Devices on the ICS Network

IT devices and their ability to become infected with malware and threaten the ICS assets were a major part of our discussion in Chapter 2. Here, we will briefly review that proposition from the perspective of the ICS vulnerabilities generated by the presence of IT devices within the ICS network. Devices such as desktop computers and servers that originate in the IT world are not uncommon elements within an ICS network. These devices all run well-known and well-compromised platforms such as Windows or Linux. These devices also possess substantial processing power and memory and become ideal staging points for an attack on ICS-specific devices such as PLCs and RTUs. It is not the 1.1%[16] of known system vulnerabilities attributed to ICS that will result in a successful attack, but the risk associated with the other 98.9% of available vulnerabilities associated with the IT system on the ICS network.

IT devices on the ICS network can serve as a staging point for attack by being compromised and operated by a remote entity through tools that get installed as part of the compromise. Through this means, IT devices on the ICS network can become Trojan horses and allow malicious entities to undertake any of the exploits against any of the mentioned vulnerability classes: DoV/DoC, LoV/LoC, and MoV/MoC. Alternately, IT devices on the ICS network can victimize ICS through collateral damage (as per Chapter 2).

Increasingly, the nature and mode of operations of malware involve the automated scanning and searching for new victims' machines. Similarly, many forms of malware will immediately start to consume massive amounts of network resources through activities such as generating spam or possibly attempting to transfer all data from the device off-site, for assessment and analysis purposes. IT malware may not necessarily target ICS assets such as PLCs and RTUs, but they certainly target the IT devices in the ICS network. To the extent that IT devices are compromised by modern malware, the resulting collateral damage to ICS on the same network could be substantial.

Interdependency with IT

Many of the ICS command and control workstations and the data historians are based on standard operating systems and platforms, such as Windows and Unix. (See the discussion in Chapter 1 about ICS architecture and IP convergence.) These platforms are in turn vulnerable to the wide and ever-expanding range of attacks against IT systems. This is the most viable and probable attack vector against ICS, through their IT interface. (Chapter 2 considers the interdependency with IT and assesses the level of threat against the IT systems of ICS user organizations to be a key indicator of the threat against ICS security.)

Interdependency with IT, or at the very least mandated interfaces with IT systems, is not a situation that is going to go away or moderate unless regulatory regimes evolve that start to prohibit or restrict these interfaces in very specific manners. There is too much business advantage to having ICS visible from the business systems, and the real-time nature of trading systems in commodities, manufactured goods, and energy will drive this integration even further.

Even for systems that have been deliberately designed and are intended to be separate, an assumption that ICS and IT systems are effectively segregated is fraught. That fact that they are both using common networking protocols and identical network elements (switches and routers) means that an IT device can be introduced, because of their common use of technology. While safeguards like network access controls may provide obstacles to purely accidental introduction of IT systems within ICS environments, they can do little to prevent an otherwise innocent and determined technician from trying to get a job done, when he needs access to the ICS network for his laptop. Perhaps he cloned a MAC address from an HMI terminal, or perhaps an ICS administrator gives his laptop temporary access through an ad hoc wireless connection; no matter, once that interface is possible, the world of IT vulnerabilities can have a direct impact.

Green Network Stacks

Green is used in this case to reflect immature and poorly tested network protocols and IP network software (stacks) that appear in ICS devices from vendors rushing to market with Ethernet and IP versions of existing products. Or vendors that still consider their products to be isolated from the badness of the business networks and Internet generally, and do not engage in extensive security testing.

The worst should be assumed about the network stacks incorporated within ICS devices such as PLCs and RTU; they should be considered fragile and prone to failure under even mildly abnormal conditions. Corrupted or deliberately "crafted packets" with unusual flags or inappropriate data lengths/types have all been shown to impact ICS in the previously discussed class of the taxonomy: DoV/DoC, LoV/LoC, and MoV/MoC.

ICS network stacks are also notorious for poor management of fluctuating traffic volumes on the network, and especially high traffic volumes. Recall that ICS protocols have been ported to IP networking, but were originally and typically intended to use only moderate amounts of network bandwidth—measurable in hundreds or thousands of bits per second, not millions of bits per second. Similarly, the ICS protocol stacks were designed for the expected, not the unexpected. Encounters with protocols beyond the limited types they were designed to manage are frequently fatal. Finally, common TCP operations like packet fragmentation are actually unusual in UDP-dominated ICS communications; as a result, the ICS network stacks tend to respond poorly to fragments.

Protocol Inertia

Related closely to the issue of green network stacks (poorly implemented and tested IP networking) on ICS devices is the issue of congenitally weak ICS protocols that not only remain in use, but also continue to be actively deployed: this is protocol inertia; it is hard to stop the momentum of operational conventions and protocols alike that have been in use for an extended period of time.

Many of the original ICS-specific protocols, such as Siemens H1, Modbus, Profibus, and others, are in active service because the devices they support are in active service and may remain so for years to come: this is a matter of their life cycle not being complete and the costs of replacement being prohibitive. Alternately, the business cases and risk analysis associated with the continued operational use of the protocols have not been proven to the satisfaction of management. This is a situation we hope to support the remedy of in this book!

However, ICS protocol vulnerabilities need not be limited only to legacy or old ICS deployments from another time and another engineering era. There are also cases of insecure protocols being used even in modern, green-field deployments of ICS. One of the best instances of this is the continued and widespread use of the Open Process Control (OPC).[17] OPC is based upon Microsoft DCOM technology, and leverages the security and authentication technique native to DCOM. OPC continues to be popular and deployed because it is a simple and standardized means of interconnecting multiple vendor products.

The challenge with the popularity of OPC is that the native DCOM security controls have been compromised to the point that it is rarely ever used anymore in the IT world. Similarly, it has been noted that even though ICS best practices from organizations like ISA recommend OPC be used only with security controls active, most deployments do not even employ the basic, available DCOM controls.[18] Rather, they prefer to deploy without security controls in place because this requires that additional Windows authentication infrastructure be deployed—adding cost and complexity. Not only that, but the presence of these new IT elements in the ICS environment again increased the vulnerabilities associated with the IT-ICS interface. Is it a good idea to bring more notoriously vulnerable systems into a fragile environment? Is the cure (expensive to maintain, vulnerable Windows systems) worse than the symptoms? It would appear that at least a substantial number of ICS practitioners using OPC without security see this as part of the case.

Additionally, authentication capabilities within the OPC/DCOM feature set can introduce latency into ICS communications, a condition to be generally avoided except as a last resort. Latency with OPC security might be not only induced in the time it takes for authentication tokens to traverse the network, but also impacted by the availability of the Windows authentication devices themselves. If the Windows servers used for authentication are an integral part of the ICS, they will probably need to be high-availability systems that will not stop working if a hard disk crashes or a network interface dies, thus increasing the expense of secure OPC further. For these reasons, ICS engineers will continue to deploy OPC without security controls. The solution is probably to stop using OPC.

Perhaps the most important piece of information to be drawn from this vulnerability associated with protocol inertia is that security controls will be resisted if they must be deployed through reconfiguration of existing ICS devices or the deployment of new (and expensive) points of failure within the ICS infrastructure.

Limited Processing Power and Memory Size

Unlike IT assets, ICS-specific devices such as PLCs and RTUs have been designed with very limited processing power and memory adequate for their intended purposes. These features allow for physically smaller footprints, robust designs to support long lifetimes, and lower-cost deployment and maintenance costs. Such factors are more important to ICS than to IT, which has large requirements for processing, storage, and manipulation of data on board the device.

Another advantage of simple devices is that the risk of administrative errors associated with management and configuration is diminished: the fewer operations there are available to operators, the lower the likelihood of security-critical operator errors.

But, there has been a security cost associated with the pursuit of small, efficient, cheap, and simple to manage devices: these devices cannot generally be upgraded, patched, or hardened. They do not possess the necessary flexibility in either their hardware or software to implement security enhancements or changes. As a result, implementing better security controls and safeguards at the network endpoints (ICS devices like PLCs and RTUs) frequently requires that these devices be replaced. In addition, replacing these devices—even if that were an affordable option—would require that the product be shut down. An on top of all this, as previously mentioned, the lack of testing environments means that the deployment of new devices to support greater security could possess a wide range of uncertainties associated with in-field, operational performance. This is not to say that anyone is upgrading security ICS based on educated guesses, but the rigor and acceptance testing processes that an ICS practitioner would naturally want to apply cannot in all cases be practically applied, leaving doubts.

CPU utilization management is rudimentary on most ICS devices, and overwhelming the CPU to invoke denial and loss events has proven to be a potential attack vector. While a typical IT operating system has the ability to place limits on the memory and CPU time allocated to a process, such as a network stack or given application, ICS devices do not generally possess this level of control. Therefore, the simplest brute force/rate-based event (attack) on a network interface can consume so much CPU time that other processes start to fail. Ideally, manufacturers should enable limiting and process priority on an ICS device operating system—a long-standing capability in the IT world. ICS devices need to ensure that they do not take memory and processing time away from critical control processes. Similarly, the data buffers on many ICS endpoint devices are not implemented with security in mind. Before any data are moved to a buffer, the size of the data and the buffer should be compared. If the data are larger than the buffer, a buffer overflow may occur, which can lead to a host of security vulnerabilities. Again, these are well-known attacks with well-known remedies in modern IT systems and in modern program development practices, but the solutions cannot be deployed on the ICS devices with their limited processing and memory profiles. So other solutions to these vulnerabilities need to be sought beyond the endpoint.

Some proposals to protect "simple" endpoint devices in the future without increasing the cost of complexity are presented in the last chapter.

Storms/DOS of Various Forms

"Packet storms" and denial of service (DOS) attacks are about flooding devices with larger than normal amounts of traffic. The intent of these storms may be to consume all bandwidth—a primitive but effective brute force approach. Other forms of storms will generate large volumes of processing by the device as it tries to keep up with semicomplete requests for connections to information. Storms and DOS attacks can come from just one antagonistic device, and need not be many. Distributed denial of service attacks (DDOS) are the bugbear of the Internet in 2011, but require dozens to millions of infected devices under coordinated control. DDOS (versus DOS) attacks are less of a direct threat to ICS unless the ICS has elements such as endpoints using the open Internet for command and control (C&C), in which case the C&C channel might be cut off by a DDOS attack. Otherwise, single compromised devices are more likely to commit DOS-like attacks from the ICS network or from adjacent, internal networks.

Many of the known, successful attacks in the categories DoV/DoC and LoV/LoC are enabled by rate-based vulnerabilities within the network stacks of the ICS endpoint devices. Specifically, these devices will fail both temporarily or in a sustained manner if the rates at which data are sent to them vary too quickly or exceed thresholds. Similarly, ICS devices will not necessarily react in the same manner with all types of packets. For instance, legitimate packets at any rate may not generate a failure, but crafted packets or simply packets with other, non-ICS protocols, may result in failures at either the IP communications interface of the I/O interface as discussed earlier in this chapter.

Figure 3.11 shows the breakdown of rate-dependent versus independent DoV/DoC, LoV/LoC vulnerabilities as categorized by Wurldtech in 2009.[19] The conclusion from this breakdown is that detection and controlling traffic spikes and anomalies on ICS networks are absolutely key to security.

Fuzzing

Fuzzing refers to the security assessment technique of pushing nearly random forms of packets and packet contents at devices to see how they respond, and if the response results in some sort of DoV/DoC, LoV/LoC situation. Fuzzers send packets that do not conform to protocol specifications. The intent of these tests is to determine how the devices handle invalid packets. Variations that fuzzers may utilize include invalid packet and payload sizes, invalid flags, and even entirely legitimate packets with gibberish payloads of the correct size and possibly even the correct format.

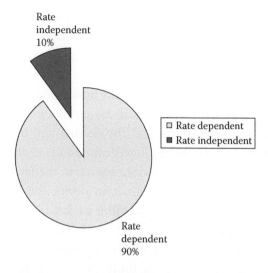

Figure 3.11 Rate dependent versus rate independent vulnerabilities in ICS endpoints.

Fuzzing can be both deliberate and accidental. Under the heading of "deliberate fuzzing," purpose-built test equipment can be bought. These testers will take well-known legacy protocols that have been ported to IP and start to play with the headers, payload, command set, packet sizes, and any other variable imaginables. Under the heading "accidental fuzzing" would be naturally occurring conditions where network traffic is corrupted in a nondeterministic, stochastic manner, meaning in a random way. The causes of such corruption would most frequently be electron magnetic interference close to cables or conduits. Such interference is common in the ICS environment and is generally taken into account during design and deployment. But the electromagnetic environment is subject to frequent change: movement of walls, equipment, or even filing cabinets can substantially change the amount of interference that a network segment is subjected to. As a result, a change in an operational environment with high degrees of electromagnetism can impact network error rates and corruption, and result in an unintentional fuzzing attack on ICS.

MITM and Packet Injection

Man-in-the-middle attacks are well understood in the IT world and have a distinct place in the ICS security world through the manipulation of view (MoV) and manipulation of control (MoC) vulnerabilities. MITM vulnerabilities in the IT world can be exploited from a variety of different points between the source and destination of a packet of information. They can occur on the source devices, where a packet might be intercepted before it leaves the device, altered, and then sent to the destination. MITM might also occur on and off the network segments between the source and the destination, but requires that routing or switching tables be altered/compromised or misconfigured to allow the packet from a malicious source to the target destination. Finally, it is possible that a destination device (i.e., historian) may be compromised such that an incoming packet is altered before it is passed to the recipient application (i.e., an ERP system).

In an ICS MITM situation, it is highly unlikely that an ICS end-point device can be compromised for interception purposes because of the limited processing power of these devices. Therefore the MITM would likely need to come from either the network or the destination device, such as an HMI or control terminal. Most ICS networks, unlike IT networks, which frequently and increasingly depend on the Internet for core connectivity to partners, suppliers, and even internal networks, do not rely upon routing over public networks. Therefore exploiting MITM vulnerabilities will require that an internal network element be severely misconfigured or compromised and controlled by a malicious entity. Since network elements like switches and routers do not themselves have sufficient resources to support an MITM application capable of altering packets in real time, threat entities would have to use an IT device to execute the MITM attack.

In the end, the MITM attack vector and the MoV/MoC threat is largely about controlling IT devices and their interfaces to the ICS network.

Packet injection is a far simpler attack on ICS because it does not require that packets be redirected, altered, and then resent to their destinations. Because so much of ICS traffic is UDP based or lacks any real form of authentication or security, packet injection can be very effective; all that is required is a device on the network that can inject the packets with a fake source and the destination address of the target. This device might be an entirely malicious device placed there for this purpose, or more likely, it may be an IT device or platform that has been compromised.

Packet injection can involve packets to either the ICS endpoint device or the SCADA or DCS infrastructures, such as a historian or a control room workstation. These packets can be used for purposes such as sending false instructions to an ICS device (MoC) or false readings to a SCADA or DCS infrastructure (MoV). Both of these are potentially highly dangerous threats as previously discussed.

Packet injection can also become a pure storming or DDOS attack, simply through escalation of the volume of the packet to the point where the ICS endpoint starts to fall into any one of the other described states.

Summary

The tools and techniques discussed in this chapter were related to the vulnerabilities associated with ICS and how they might be recognized. We have not spent time discussing highly system-specific vulnerabilities, since these are (1) largely not known at this time due to the small amount of research that has been done, and (2) ICS vulnerabilities are not just about endpoint devices but are systemic. For instance, the unique combination of device types, network fragility, and the type and number of IT interfaces makes for unique vulnerability profiles.

One way to use the technical discussions in this chapter is as a filter, helping to narrow down and identify the vulnerability that might be most important to the ICS under consideration, versus focusing on specific vulnerabilities that happen to be "popular" through hype and FUD (fear, uncertainly, and doubt) in the media.

Endnotes

1. Purdue Enterprise Reference Architecture (PERA), http://www.pera.net/.
2. *Open-loop control* means commands are issued without observing the resulting state in order to adjust inputs. In other words, there is no feedback loop; if a loop is not closed it is open, which actually makes it a nonloop as opposed to the oxymoron *open loop*.
3. See Traders Profit from Computers Set at High Speeds, *New York Times*, July 24, 2009; also Rise of the Machines, *The Economist*, July 30, 2009.
4. High-Speed Traders—Spread Betting, *The Economist*, August 12. 2010, http://www.economist.com/node/16792950/print.
5. As per NIST 800-53 guidance related to recommended control classes for IT systems, management, operational, and technical control frameworks are useful and widely used for the management of security programs. ISO

standards such as 27002 included this full range of controls, but elected to organize them according to control area (IE, access control, personnel security) rather than by control class.

6. Jeff Dagle, *Potential Mitigation Strategies for the Common Vulnerabilities of Control Systems Identified by the NERC Control Systems Security Working Group*, U.S. DOE, 2005.
7. As determined by a full-text search for the terms *SCADA*, *ICS*, *RTU*, *PLC*, *Rockwell*, *Modbus*, or *Aurora*, common vulnerabilities and exposures, http://cve.mitre.org/.
8. Distribution of INL results, http://www.digitalbond.com/index.php/2009/09/29/distribution-of-inl-assessment-results/.
9. Ibid., Kevin Yoo.
10. Wurldtech blog, Common Vulnerabilities and Exposure for the Rest of Us—February 2009, http://www.wurldtech.com/blog/?cat=24.
11. Spanish grid blacked out by hackers, http://www.cnn.com/2007/US/09/26/power.at.risk/index.html.
12. Chemical Safety Board, http://www.csb.gov.
13. CSB safety video: explosion at BP refinery, http://www.youtube.com/watch?v=c9JY3eT4cdM.
14. U.S. video shows hacker hit on power grid, http://www.chinadaily.com.cn/world/2007-09/27/content_6139437.htm. (Ironically, it is a Chinese publication that appears to have the fullest coverage of this story, while INL—the U.S. DoD institution that conducted the test—has no obviously referenced material on these tests.)
15. *Information Week*, http://www.informationweek.com/story/showArticle.jhtml?articleID=205901631.
16. Ibid., 25.
17. See http://www.opcfoundation.org.
18. Sean Leonard, *OPC Security: Controlling Access to Critical System Data*, ISA, 2009.
19. Ibid., 34.

4

RISK ASSESSMENT TECHNIQUES

Introduction

In the previous chapters, we reviewed the threat and vulnerabilities that ICS face. In this chapter we will turn our attention toward the issue of what to do with this information. Understanding vulnerabilities is helpful but does not provide guidance about which vulnerabilities are more important than others. Understanding threats facing ICS is also important—critically so—because it allows practitioners to narrow down the range of vulnerabilities that must be managed. Combining our understanding of vulnerabilities and threats and applying specific knowledge about the potential severity of impacts results in a process of risk assessment.

There are many methodologies for ICS risk assessment. These methodologies may distinguish themselves in a variety of ways. For instance, they may recommend different ICS threat lists, or they may specialize in the assessment of certain types of ICS vulnerabilities. They may be tuned for specific industries or even specific sorts of ICS infrastructure. As a starting point, it is appropriate to quickly review the more widely known ICS risk assessment methodologies, since these are also widely accepted as decent starting points for practitioners. In other words, they are fundamental considerations that any practitioner should be aware of before moving on to more experimental techniques, which may provide different and deeper insights.

After reviewing a range of existing ICS risk assessment techniques, we will undertake a discussion related to new, evolving, and novel assessment methods. The purpose of this chapter is not to merely review existing systems for risk assessment associated with ICS, but to expose and promote new systems that are building up the state of practice in ICS risk management.

Contemporary ICS Security Analysis Techniques

The following ICS security analysis techniques represent both commonly cited approaches and some of the best-known approaches. This is not an inventory of all the available approaches to assessing ICS security; however, this sample is broadly representative of the range of current practices in ICS security assessment.

In most cases, the techniques and practices most widely propagated for assessing ICS vulnerabilities are reworked IT vulnerability methodologies, and while they may be broadly recognized, it is difficult to assess how widely they are used by ICS practitioners.

Entities such as the U.S. Department of Homeland Security (DHS) and the U.S. National Institute of Standards and Technology (NIST) successfully invested in and developed this first generation of ICS risk assessment guidance starting around 2003–2004; however, *significant opportunities for improvement remain* and are greatly needed because the state of practice in ICS security was advanced only a little by these early efforts relative to where it needs to be. For instance, these early efforts at assessment methodologies frequently assumed that the balance of confidentiality, integrity, and availability requirements was consistent from IT to ICS—a perception repeatedly exposed in this book as inaccurate if not dangerous.

North American Electricity Reliability Council (NERC)

> NERC's mission is to improve the reliability and security of the bulk power systems in the United States, Canada and parts of Mexico. The organization aims to do that, not only by enforcing compliance with mandatory Reliability Standards, but also by acting as a "force for good"—a catalyst for positive change whose role includes shedding light on system weaknesses, helping industry participants operate and plan to the highest possible level, and communicating Examples of Excellence throughout the industry.[1]

It is instructive to review NERC's approach to vulnerability assessment and risk management because its members are prime examples of large-scale ICS users with significant consequences associated with system compromise. NERC is also one of the most high-profile users of ICS in North America and proactive with regard to security, due equally to public pressure and an innate understanding of the potential impacts on public safety. It many ways, NERC might be expected to be at the vanguard of security assessment techniques and be among the security leaders in the ICS user community.

NERC Security Guidelines for the Electricity Sector: Vulnerability and Risk Assessment[2] consists of a five-page document first published in 2002 and is as of the date of this writing, unrevised. NERC's guidance for assessing security of ICS consists of four steps on one page:

1. Identification of asset and loss impacts
2. Identification and analysis of vulnerabilities
3. Assessment of risk and the determination of priorities for the protection of critical assets
4. Identification of countermeasures, their costs, and trade-offs

However, NERC has also published its own critical infrastructure protection (CIP) standards, known as NERC-CIP in the industry. NERC-CIP is a body of guidance related to issues such as:

1. Sabotage reporting (updated February 2010)
2. Critical cyber asset identification (updated December 2009)
3. Security management controls (updated December 2009)
4. Cyber security—personnel and training (updated December 2009)
5. Cyber security—electronic security perimeter (updated December 2009)
6. Physical security of cyber assets (updated February 2010)
7. Cyber security—incident reporting (updated December 2009)
8. Cyber security—recovery plans (updated December 2009)

Within the body of this document, NERC provides additional guidance related to risk assessment within CIP-002-3: *Critical Cyber Asset Identification.*

The guidance in CIP-002 is apparently limited to requiring that responsible entities "shall identify and document a risk-based assessment methodology." Therefore any assessment methodology may be adopted as long as it is written down and executed consistently. Similarly, NERC-CIP only requires that "critical" systems be assessed.

If a system is deemed noncritical through deliberate or accidental omissions in the identification process, then the assessment may be manipulated by managers seeking merely to report a positive result.

National Institute of Standards and Technology (NIST)

NIST 800-82: *Guide to Industrial Control System Security* was first published in September 2008. This document represents the first specific effort related to ICS undertaken by NIST. NIST 800-82 recommends that established security and vulnerability testing methodologies can be adapted to ICS environments, and the same tools for testing can be applied; however, NIST cautions that ICS devices are susceptible to failure and overload as a result of basic tests, and provides some guidance on how to modify established testing methods for ICS environments. The limit of this guidance can be found in Table 4.1, which is a replication directly from NIST 800-82.

In addition, NIST provides supplemental guidance related to the security of ICS within appendix information to the oft-cited 800-53v3: *Recommended Security Controls for Federal Systems*, specifically, "Appendix I: Industrial Control Systems—Security Controls, Enhancements, and Supplemental Guidance." This additional guidance is focused on adopting the 800-53 IT system controls to ICS environments. To the extent that additional guidance on security assessment is

Table 4.1 NIST Security Assessment Guidance

TO BE IDENTIFIED	USUAL IT ACTION	SUGGESTED ICS ACTION
• Hosts, nodes, and networks	• Ping sweep (e.g., nmap)	• Examine router configuration files or route tables • Perform physical verification (chasing wires) • Conduct passive network listening or use intrusion detection (e.g., snort) on the network • Specify a subset of IP addresses to be programmatically scanned
• Services	• Port scan (e.g., nmap)	• Do local port verification (e.g., netstat) • Scan a duplicate, development, or test system on a nonproduction network
• Vulnerabilities within a service	• Vulnerability scan (e.g., nessus)	• Perform local banner grabbing with version lookup in Common Vulnerabilities and Exposures (CVE) • Scan a duplicate, development, or test system on a nonproduction network

provided, 800-53 advises that ICS environments should be duplicated for testing where possible, due to the fragility of the systems.[3]

NIST 800-82 and NIST 800-53v3 are the tools recommended by earlier versions of ISA-99 Part 4: *Technical Security Requirements for Industrial Automation and Control Systems* for assessing target assurance levels and risks; however, subsequent versions and current drafts of the evolving ISA-99 standards are moving in distinct directions from NIST.

It should be noted that while NIST and the U.S. federal government are obviously concerned parties, and accountable for public safety, when it comes to ICS security, NIST and the federal government are limited users of ICS themselves. The implication of this observation is that the differentiation of ICS security requirements may be only partially expressed in guidelines from NIST, versus those from user associations and organizations.

ICS devices will potentially find IPv6 environments a challenge for at least two reasons. First, because the evolving lower-level communications protocols do not easily accommodate a IPv6 world. Second, the requirements for processing power associated with IPv6 and then the higher-level protocols like TCP or UDP impose a burden that may exhaust such devices. Exhaustion may be in the form of power exhaust (which would require service or replacement) or processor exhaustion (which could present denial of service-type vulnerabilities!). Part of the solution to these challenges will likely be chip-based processing of IP and even TCP headers for ICS and other smart devices. Chip-based processing is much more power efficient and faster than software or firmware approaches, which use the general/central processing unit. Increasingly, chip makers are shrinking the IP and TCP "off-load engines" they make for chips, and these engines are finding their way onto the new generation of low-power chips. The question then becomes a matter of whether or not the IP and TCP/UDP stacks embedded onto chips in ICS and smart devices are hardened properly to withstand the range of attacks we have discussed in this book.

Department of Homeland Security (DHS) ICS Risk Assessment Processes

DHS, through its National Cyber Security Division, has funded the research and development of ICS security test beds, methodologies, and tools through its Control Systems Security Program.[4] A substantial amount of this has funded the ICS security concentrations at the Idaho National Laboratory (INL).[5] INL was established in 1949 and is a publicly funded engineering national laboratory dedicated to supporting the U.S. Department of Energy's missions in nuclear and energy research, science, and national defense. The mission of INL is to ensure the nation's energy security through safe, competitive, and sustainable energy systems and unique national and homeland security capabilities. The attacks of 2001 brought attention to the potential threats associated with critical infrastructure and energy in particular. INL was at that time directed to apply resources specifically into a supervisory control and data acquisition (SCADA)/ICS security program, under the National Strategy to Secure Cyberspace of 2002.

Without specifically enumerating them, INL appears to be supporting, or at least investigating, multiple distinct approaches to ICS security assessment: a national SCADA test bed program, a published vulnerability assessment methodology, a metrics-based assessment process, and an assessment system called ideal-based metrics.

INL National SCADA Test Bed Program (NSTB): Control System Security Assessment

The test bed assessment process is highly flexible and may be tailored to the mutual interests of the industry partner. The typical process includes the following sequence:

- Establish agreement that defines the working relationship (scope, personnel, equipment, facilities, cost sharing) and ensures protection of sensitive information.
- Obtain equipment and training from the industry partner.
- Set up equipment with support from the industry partner.
- Perform tests to identify cyber vulnerabilities.
- Provide detailed test report to industry partner.
- Issue report suitable for public release to Web sites, conferences, and users' groups

A key objective of the NSTB program is to share information obtained through assessments with potentially impacted stakeholders, with an emphasis on asset owners and users. However, it is recognized that much of the information obtained in assessments is business sensitive to the industry partner whose system or technology has been assessed. The program works with the industry partner to determine what information obtained or derived from the assessment process is appropriate for disclosure outside the partnership, and to identify an appropriate format and forum for disclosure. No information is released without the written concurrence of the industry partner.

INL Vulnerability Assessment Methodology

A vulnerability assessment is often distinct from a risk assessment, but is also a prerequisite for a risk assessment. While we discussed vulnerabilities in a previous chapter, we will cover the INL vulnerability assessment process alongside the overall risk assessment process here, to provide a complete versus fragmented picture.

INL has two specific focuses related to ICS security testing:

- Test bed design
- Target of evaluation (TOE) methodology support

While INL supports a test bed laboratory itself (as described above), this lab is insufficient to meet the requirements of the entire nation, and is for demonstration rather than delivery of services to clients. INL recommends to ICS users that they create their own test beds and provides the following guidance:

- Replicate all ICS devices as exactly as possible, not just devices considered vital or susceptible to attack.
- Mirroring the connections to external systems is vital when replicating the ICS configuration, including Internet connections and connections to supplier and partner sites.
- Replicate firewalls and intrusion detection systems (IDS) devices on the perimeter.
- If a historian database is typically placed in the corporate network, that configuration should be implemented in the target system.

TOE methodology guidance is not provided in a specific, step-by-step document because ICS design and architectures can and do differ dramatically from system to system. The following testing guidance is provided by INL:

- Penetration testing must be conducted from a machine that is not part of the SCADA system unless otherwise defined in the assessment plan (i.e., an insider threat or malware).
- The test bed must be returned to its original state after each of the tests listed below and any other tests the practitioner chooses to apply. All devices should be reset or restarted according to manufacturer specifications and returned to a stable operational state comparable to the operational environment.
- The following forms of testing should be performed as part of the testing regime:
  - Port scans should be undertaken as an entry-level test. Many ICS devices can be especially sensitive to simple port scans.
  - Man-in-the-middle (MITM) attacks can be accomplished with access to network elements like switches or routers, with a device tapped in line between the control console and the control device. MITM attacks that try to change or nullify legitimate commands should be tested.
  - Software debuggers should review running ICS source code for flaws. ICS source code software may be obtainable from a number of sources, ranging from compromised vendor systems to mishandled escrow agreements. The assumption should be made that adversaries have access to ICS source code, and vulnerabilities can become visible using off-the-shelf development tools.
  - Static code testing: Disassemble/reverse engineer code. ICS software packages may be obtainable from a number of sources, ranging from vendor samples to online upgrade distributions and others. The assumption should be made that adversaries have access to ICS software, and vulnerabilities can become visible using off-the-shelf disassemble tools.
  - Exploitation testing should be performed using open-source tools and exploitation kits associated with ICS platforms.

- Custom crafted packet and exploitation testing. ICS exploit kits are not available for all ICS platforms. However, ICS testing can also occur through custom-developed exploits by practitioners knowledgeable of the ICS protocols. Custom crafted packets may include things like invalid data, buffer overflows, or simple IP spoofing.
- Fuzzing (invalid input sent to devices). Fuzzing consists of a wide variety of data sent over the wire to ICS (or other) devices, which may or may not be contained within a legitimate protocol. Alternately, the protocol may be deliberately broken in a near-random sequence of manners. The point of fuzzing is to understand the resilience of the devices to not only crafted attacks (which were not considered deliberately), but also to random events on the network, possibly originating from legitimate sources.

INL Metrics-Based Reporting for Risk Assessment[6]

INL initially investigated the use of mathematical expressions of attack probability for understanding risks to ICS. The variables that INL considered were:

1. Whether the facility is a target (assumed as 1 or yes/true)
2. Chances of an attack being launched (versus imagined/considered/planned)
3. Likelihood of an ICS perimeter breech; probability of critical nodes in the system capable of inflicting damage being breeched
4. Chance that breeching a critical system will result in a direct consequence

However, this effort was suspended when it was decided that trying to understand or estimate the probability of attack was too difficult given the lack of information and quantitative data associated with threats. For instance, verified attacks on ICS are few and far between, and there are no statistics on attacks that were attempted but failed or were aborted. This is likely an intractable problem in the physical world; however, as Chapter 2 in this book book outlines, there are approaches for the cyber world, which makes it possible to measure failed and aborted attacks on ICS as a possible indicator of threat attack probability.

After further consideration, INL has started pursuing a different approach where risk reduction metrics were sought, using the following variables:

1. Whether the facility is a target (assumed as 1 or yes/true)
2. Capability level of the threat agent (from 1 to 4)
3. Increase or decrease in controls and safeguards
4. Chance that breeching a critical system will result in a direct consequence

Similar to the case with the attack probability formulation, INL reached the conclusion that attack surfaces are extremely large and ICS are so complex that estimation in quantitative measures cannot be done exhaustively, and further work is required to logically and consistently reduce attack surfaces to manageable sizes. Furthermore, consequence variables (impact associated with the threat agent successfully exploiting a vulnerability) have multiple dimensions and levels of detail. For instance, consequences can be measured as dollars, injury, loss of life, environmental damage, and reputation/goodwill. Applying quantitative measures for even these high-level variables also requires further study.

Ideal-Based Risk Assessment and Metrics

Ideal-based metrics is another notable ICS risk assessment process proposed by INL research starting in 2007.[7] It is notable because ideal-based risk assessment is certainly a novel approach and worth mentioning given the intense complexity of ICS and the difficulty in arriving at even broadly correct risk assessments using the same or similar modes as are traditionally applied.

According to Boyer and McQueen, with "ideal-based metrics one can make a positive statement-of-measure for cybersecurity protection. This is in contrast to the use of *argumentum ad ignorantiam* where just because you have no evidence of a protection breach implies a fully protected [ICS]. This combination of mitigating strategies and a known scalar measurement system for [ICS] is the correct method of establishing the known level of protection.... The ideal-based metrics are agreements on the attributes of an ideal cybersecurity system and then assessing how closely the considered system approaches the ideal."

In other words, ICS risk assessors do not know what they do not know about ICS and should therefore calculate risk backwards from an ideal state by assessing how far a target of evaluation is from this state. At the very least, this will provide a minimum reading of risk, since it does not start with the premise that the most likely threats can be enumerated. Instead, the ideal-based system, they say, creates the ideal ICS security architecture, including the defined metrics, and then assesses against how much of the ideal is reflected in the current system and perhaps in future planned improvements.

As a fresh approach, the ideal-based system certainly possesses merit, but it also immediately leads to complex new challenges, perhaps on par or even exceeding the challenges presented by more traditional ICS risk assessment techniques. Ideal-based assessment would require that a scoring system be developed that allows a target ICS to accumulate points up to 100% of the ideal system, or fall measurably short of this goal. This in turn requires that weights and individual scores be applied to discrete controls and safeguards, and points be awarded on the basis of their existence or absence. Effort would clearly be required to propose how this would be done in a quantitative and consistent manner, because different individuals will score differently. Ideal-based risk assessment and metrics will also need to address the economics law of diminishing returns: in this instance, the closer one approaches an ideal or perfectly secure ICS, the more expensive each incremental improvement becomes the closer you approach the ideal state! Eventually, an ideal-based system may require work by standards groups to establish agreed-upon ordinal metrics or points-systems for specific security controls like IDS, FW, network monitoring, and so forth.

CCSP Cyber Security Evaluation Tool (CSET)[8]

The Control System Cyber Security Program (CCSP) under DHS has developed and made available for free the CSET, which is a software-based tool developed in combination with the National Institute of Standards and Technology (NIST) and represents a software interface for doing ICS security assessments against recognized industry standards. CSSP also runs the ICS-CERT (Cyber Emergency Response Team), which provides useful insights into documented and known ICS vulnerabilities. This intelligence may allow for greater insight and assessment of the likelihood that ICS vulnerabilities may be exploited.

CSSP describes its tool in this way: "CSET is a desktop software tool that guides users through a step-by-step process to assess their control system and information technology network security practices against recognized industry standards. The output from CSET is a prioritized list of recommendations for improving the cybersecurity posture of the organization's enterprise and industrial control cyber systems. The tool derives the recommendations from a database of cybersecurity standards, guidelines, and practices. Each recommendation is linked to a set of actions that can be applied to enhance cybersecurity controls."

Presumably the standards applied include NIST 800-53, which is also the basis of NIST 800-82, and hopefully the work of ISA-99. As a result, CSET would appear to be a derivative application of IT security standards rather than a unique ICS security methodology itself.

U.S. Department of Energy: Electricity Sector Cyber Security Risk Management Process Guideline

In September 2011, during the copyedit stage of this book, the U.S. Department of Energy (DOE) released a risk management methodology which is ostensibly targeted at the electricity sector. This methodology is possibly intended to fill the gap identified earlier in this chapter related to the NERC security guidelines which are rather vague in their guidance around risk assessment processes, other than to say that they should be employed.

The DOE risk management guidance is the latest and possibly the best of the risk assessment methodologies proposed for ICS user entities for several reasons. First, the DOE methodology recognized that there are different forms of risk in an organization (even though they focus on electricity products). The forms of risk identified include *Organizational, Mission and Business Process,* and *Information Technology and Industrial Control Systems (ICS).* Organizational risks as defined in the DOE methodology appears analogous to a more common notion of "business" risks and requirements which have to do with such things that are regulatory and contractual obligations, compliance, reporting and governance, and identifying the enterprise level risks. Mission and Technology risks flow from organizational risks. Most important in the DOE methodology is the relationship between these realms of Organizational, Mission, and Technical risk: all top-level risks, Organizational risks must be addressed by controls in the lower Mission level, and eventually, all Mission level risks addressed at the Technical level. In this manner, risk management is integrated through the organization and business cases based on risks that can be traced from technical sources to top-level business requirements.

The last thing we will note related to the merit of the DOE methodology is that it stipulated what amounts to the use of both qualitative and quantitative metrics for assessing risk. As we have mentioned several times, a common weakness of risk assessment methods is the reliance on purely qualitative measurements of risk which prove unconvincing at the executive level. For instance, at the top Organizational tier, security metrics may include quantifiable vulnerabilities like value-at-risk, potential sanctions and fines, and cost of capital impacts. At the Mission tier, metrics may include the quantified degree of compliance with security standards and policies and exception rates ("100 out of 130 controls in place"). Finally, at the lowest, Technical level metrics might include the number and duration of changes, processes, vulnerabilities detected and present in the system, monitoring and logging levels, and status report metrics.

As a result of its approach to establishing and mapping security requirements across multiple tiers of the enterprise, the DOE methodology is approaching risk management for ICS systems from a newly rigorous perspective.

Evolving Risk Assessment Processes

In this second part of the chapter we will introduce a few emerging methods and processes for assessing risks in ICS. By emerging we mean that they have been deployed and used by the authors and others in operational environments, but are not necessarily broadly known.

These emerging systems tend to have one thing in common: they represent a movement away from qualitative risk assessment toward more quantitative processes. In other words, they try and generate the risk measurements that would be repeatable: if a new person were to perform the same assessment, the results would be the same. This is not to say these assessments achieve this objective of highly accurate, reliable, and repeatable risk assessments. We are not there yet. But they are a clear reflection of the need to get away from professional opinions when dealing with ICS risks.

Consequence Matrices

ICS compromises typically involve multilevel or chained exploits, in which an attacker gains multiple insights into the system architecture and then uses this information to plan an attack. In most known cybersecurity attacks against ICS, the system's valid functions and entry points were used.

Current security disciplines focus heavily on a single-point vulnerability, but this is rarely the case for ICS. For instance, an attacker requires only one or very few vulnerabilities to compromise an entire database and access, change, or destroy sensitive information. Single-point vulnerabilities are of reduced value to ICS attackers, because ICS threats usually require more than one security failure to manifest.

A consequence matrix is a tool to visualize and assess how major elements in the ICS network might serve as access and attacks points to other assets. The benefit of using consequence matrices is that they perform the role of a more traditional statement of sensitivity (SOS) from a qualitative threat risk assessment, but represent the often overlooked and highly complex area of asset interdependencies.

Asset interdependencies as described through the consequence matrix might be the first phase of an ICS assessment, and should be undertaken whether the assessment is intended merely against a single, discrete asset, a whole plant, or an entire production system spanning many facilities and remote devices. Consequence matrices provide critical views into not only where threats and impacts can come from, but where they can go after the asset is affected. These insights start to allow for an understanding of cascading effects within ICS, which lead to outright security failures both the most pernicious and difficult to assess type of impacts.

The consequence matrix in Figure 4.1 is a sample using typical asset classes found in ICS reference architectures, such as those published by DHS and the Idaho National Laboratory (INL). Black represents

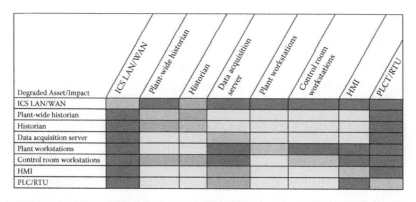

Figure 4.1 Sample consequence modeling of ICS network assets.

a high risk of attack from the asset in the column to the assets in the rows, if the column asset is compromised or accessible by threat agents. Gray indicates a medium risk of attack and white a moderate risk. (Remember, this is just an example, so we are not providing definitions of risk here.)

The consequence matrix in Figure 4.1 indicates that a particular asset imparts risk to most other assets (columns) if it is compromised: the network. Similarly, this asset (the network) is subject to threat/attack (rows) from all other assets if they are compromised. Less obvious relationships also become apparent and possibly represent more value in assessment; for instance, the relationships between workstations and data acquisition servers may not be entirely evident to assessors without this tool.

Creating a consequence matrix is a system-specific operation, with different ICS possessing different relationships between their asset elements, depending on their design and even the goods in production.

The first step in developing a consequence matrix would be the identification of the high-level assets, or at least confirming that the INL reference architecture groupings make sense. It then becomes a matter of information gathering from operational personnel to understand the interdependencies at play; probably several interviews will be required with different individuals, if not groups. But at the very least this will afford the risk assessor an invaluable opportunity to interface with operational staff to understand information that cannot be conveyed meaningfully through schematics or diagrams.

Safety Integrity Levels and Security Assurance Levels

During the 1990s a rising number of industrial incidents catalyzed a detailed review of industry safety practices and a push toward standardized levels of practice. This resulted in the Industrial Society of Automation (ISA) creating ANSI/ISA-84.00.01-1996, which defines the safety integrity levels for use in assessing safety requirements for ICS components and safety systems. The standard focuses on risk reduction through a systematic process associated with hardware faults and failures.

A safety integrity level (SIL) is a probability of mechanical failure in components. SIL is regulated by the Occupational Safety and Health Administration (OSHA). The implementation of SIL levels is not dictated, but is contributory evidence for compliance. The ambition of the standards body (ISA) promoting the SIL approach is that it too will reach the level of being considered a substantial, contributory piece of evidence toward a determination of either due care or negligence. SIL levels are probabilistic, and are established and internationalized in ISA-82, ISO 61508, and IEC 61508/511.

There are four levels of SIL: level 4 has the highest requirements for safety integrity, while level 1 has the lowest. The higher the SIL, the higher the confidence that the required safety function will operate as expected when needed over the designed operational life. IEC 61508 established the probability of unsafe failures for each SIL, as shown in Table 4.2. Table 4.2 shows the probability of failure for on-demand systems with a low-demand rate (no more than one operation per year—10^4 hours). Table 4.3 shows the probability for systems with continuous operation or a high-demand rate (no more than one per hour, and therefore increased by 10^4).[9]

The limitation of the SIL system is that it applies specifically to random hardware failures, and does not explicitly consider systemic faults and software failures or intentional actions. SIL and safety design consider

Table 4.2 SIL Levels for Low-Demand Mode

SAFETY INTEGRITY LEVEL	PROBABILITY OF FAILURE TO PERFORM SAFETY FUNCTIONS ON DEMAND
4	$\geq 10^{-5} < 10^{-4}$
3	$\geq 10^{-4} < 10^{-3}$
2	$\geq 10^{-3} < 10^{-2}$
1	$\geq 10^{-2} < 10^{-1}$

Table 4.3   SIL Levels for Continuous or High Demand

SAFETY INTEGRITY LEVEL	PROBABILITY OF DANGEROUS FAILURES PER HOUR
4	$\geq 10^{-9} < 10^{-8}$
3	$\geq 10^{-8} < 10^{-7}$
2	$\geq 10^{-7} < 10^{-6}$
1	$\geq 10^{-6} < 10^{-5}$

the results of a process hazards analysis that rates impacts and evaluates likelihood of failure on demand of controllers and safety systems, and then provides information for proper safety instrumented systems (SIS) selection to mitigate risk of hardware faults to an acceptable level.

In a sense, SIL is a risk assessment and management tool for one specific threat: random hardware failure. SILs also reflect an engineering discipline which evolved largely independent of the move toward IP-based integration, and therefore does not address intentionally malicious events (malware: viruses, worms, botnets, etc.), whether directed or the proverbial "lucky strike." Each of the safety standards, such as ISA-84 and IEC 61508 and 61511, point to the need for secure systems, but take the approach of only addressing safety threats with a measurable condition: random hardware faults.

Security Assurance Level

The security assurance level (SAL) concept has been initially defined and continues to develop in the ISA-99.00.01 and ISA-99.00.02 standards documents. SAL takes into account intentional, accidental, and internal or external threats, measuring in terms of consequence. Essentially, SAL helps round out the picture to protect ICS from a variety of different threats than SIL. It is complementary to the SIL and SIS processes, and also considers wider process risk. While SIL will consider how an ICS device performs with normal inputs, SAL considers how the software within a device will respond given unexpected inputs, whether related to protocols, payloads, or data rates, and whether accidental, random, or malicious.

There is a distinction between SIL and SAL that also makes them mutually useful and symbiotic: the majority of vulnerabilities in ICS result from systematic risks. For instance, while it is possible that a single device can fail, and that event by itself can cause a catastrophic event, it is more common to see a series of failures that cascade through a system—the combination of which generates abnormal events and resulting impacts. The system interdependency problem is compounded when direct and intentional attacks induce systematic failures at multiple levels. It is no longer possible to rely upon a single-point analysis of a particular device, because a constructed attack against modern ICS can result in failures at many levels of operation within the system.

Typically, if any process has ever gone through a safety study, there should be a wealth of information about what the most critical and dangerous failures may be; therefore the worst-case scenarios are often known. Security analysts quickly find, however, that much of the identified risk from these studies was discounted or not fully considered during process design and implementation.

The reason risk assessment information is often set aside (if available) at process design time is at least twofold:

1. The risk data were purely qualitative and not compelling/believable enough to justify changes and potentially adding cost.
2. The risk findings were presented in such a manner that they were unintelligible to management and the business case is rejected.

SAL is a systematic approach to assessing risk treatment requirements based on quantitative measures, expressed in management-level terms (SAL levels—to be covered shortly).

Safety disciplines evolved to establish target rates of occurrence of dangerous failures through the rigorous testing of ICS and SIS to arrive at quantitative metrics such as dangerous failures per hour for a given device. The results and benefits to industry have been more reliable components, but they do not effectively factor in intentional threats. So, where a safety discipline might suggest a redundant array of three SIS elements, engineers would likely select the same type of system for each redundant component. To an attacker, however, if a common mode failure is known for a given device, it is a simple matter to bypass all redundant controls by using the same deliberate attack on all instances of the control device.

SAL intends to overcome more traditional risk analysis gaps by providing a systems-oriented capability. By this means, designers can take into account additional factors in planning, implementing, and validating their systems. Additionally, SAL prescribes heavy testing and validation measures for establishing the assurance of industrial processes and networks for both performance and cyber security issues that could complicate start-up or impede effective operations.

SAL provides a description of risk associated with a given ICS component and can be scaled to an entire ICS, including enterprise operations.

SAL is broader than pure random failures of software or hardware, as it encompasses the additional disciplines of software security and assurance. SAL "aims to provide justifiable confidence that the software is free of vulnerabilities, that it functions in the intended manner and that the intended manner does not compromise the security and other required properties of the software, its environment, or the information it handles. Software assurance also aims to provide justifiable confidence that the software will remain dependable under all circumstances."[10]

For some readers, SAL may sound similar to the common criteria (CC) assessment and certification program that is available in the IT world and regularly performed on devices and software used in high-assurance environments. This is a fair observation. However, it should be noted that CC is not intended to account for impacts on the system environment, the rest of the ICS, or compliance risk. Because SAL is still under development, it is possible that this last objective is too grandiose, though SAL may possibly become an ICS relative to CC.

James Gilsinn and Ragnar Schierholz in their paper, "Security Assurance Level Vector," define four main SAL types as: target, design, achieved, and capabilities. All are related and have to do with different aspects of the security life cycle.

- *Target SAL* levels are the desired level of security for a particular system. This is usually determined by performing a risk assessment on a system and determining that it needs a particular level of security to ensure its correct operation.
- *Design SAL* levels are the planned level of security for a particular system. These SAL levels may go through multiple revisions during the design process as different countermeasures are explored to meet the target SAL levels.
- *Achieved SAL* levels are the actual level of security for a particular system. These are measured after a system is in place and are used to establish that a security system is meeting the goals that were originally set in the target SAL levels.

- *Capability SAL* levels are the security levels that systems or components can provide when properly configured. These levels state that a particular system or component is capable of meeting the target SAL levels without additional compensating controls when properly configured and integrated.[11]

Gilsinn and Schierholz relate SALs to each other, thus:

Each of these SALs is intended to be used in a different phase of the security life cycle according to the ISA99 series of standards. Starting with a target for a particular system, an organization would need to build a design that included the capabilities to achieve the desired result. In other words, the design team would first develop the target SAL necessary for a particular system. They would then design the system to meet those targets, resulting in the design SAL. As part of that design process, the designers would pick systems and components with the necessary capability SALs to meet the design SAL requirements. After the system went into operation, the actual SAL would be measured as the achieved SAL and compared to the target and design SAL.[12]

SAL-Based Assessments

While SILs can focus primarily on hardware faults and some level of software faults, SALs focus on hardware, software, network communications, and the system as a whole. Testing includes logical (protocol violations through fuzzing, exploitation techniques, and network resilience) and physical conditions (such as cable runs or operating temperatures).

SALs can be understood in the context of understanding the controllability of the process, where a difference in the currently assessed SAL and the target SAL demonstrates that an insufficient control condition can result in risk.

Achieving a SIL rating requires assigning a probability of failure to protection mechanisms within the context of a particular device and its immediate connection points, such as I/O and HMI. It must be demonstrated through device testing that the device can achieve a level of resilience against such failures and meet the desired failure rate.

SAL testing of a device requires positive testing to ensure that all functions work correctly, and also negative testing to demonstrate that any anomalous inputs, outputs, device states, conditions, or other exceptions are handled properly. Successful testing requires the following:

- The device components, communications architectures, and processing capabilities must be known.
- The designed function, including all positive and negative logic states, must be understood.
- Communications protocols and device communication design must be documented and understood with all legitimate permutations exercised.
- Exception handling (fail-safe) protocols and functionality must be tested in a suitable set of permutations.

The SAL model requires additional considerations when testing devices for specific security resiliency and protection against security violations. For instance:

- *Device stack management*—Following good design patterns, unit testing, system testing, avoiding deprecated libraries and objects, source code standards, and peer review.
- *Network protocol analysis and testing*—Communications protocols must be inspected and tested for conditions such as TCP SYN flood attacks, exploitable conditions in reliability and data transmissions, and device network communication tolerances to avoid denial of service. Testing must include bounds testing, flood/storm testing, and protocol fuzzing.
- *Security vulnerability and penetration testing*—Utilizing known security flaws or flaws discovered in earlier testing to conduct penetration testing to prove exploitable conditions and to determine mitigating controls.
- *Testing at layer 1* (physical layer of OSI) of network and input-oriented tests such as voltage spikes and sags, electromagnetic interference, and other installation and environmental factors.

Given that exhaustive, probabilistic testing is difficult due to the highly systemic nature of ICS and the component devices, software, and networks, a purely quantitative SAL rating is not appropriate and probably not practical. The currently recommended SAL rating is summarized in Table 4.4.

SAL Workflow

Figure 4.2 is a representation of a SAL workflow. Note that in the course of a SAL-based assessment, two actual SAL calculations are

Table 4.4 SAL Rating

SAL	EXAMPLES OF POTENTIAL IMPACTS	TYPICAL PROTECTION MECHANISMS
1	• Negligible to no impacts, near miss safety incidents, or minor first aid, minor process efficiency hits, limited to no quality impacts, little to no regulatory concerns.	• Minor ability required to detect unauthorized devices or process changes • Minor requirements for access control and authorization • Limited requirements for backup and recovery or configuration management
2	• Possible safety incidents (bumps, trips, falls, or injury requiring hospital visits or resulting in lost time), minor process stoppages, or efficiency hits that can be recovered before supply chain impact, recordable or reportable regulatory concerns, and so forth.	• Access control and authorization needed • Network management includes some ability to monitor and maintain network and switches • Changes in controllers are backed up and recorded in a log to facilitate rapid recovery • Some prevention against unauthorized devices and program changes • SIS used in accordance with SIL • Policy and training in line with corporate IT and other policies, some specific shop floor
3	• Safety incidents including death, dismemberment, or long-term injury, but on a limited basis of approximately 1 to 3 people. Process stoppages or efficiency hits that result in delayed orders and damage to reputation, significant increase in production and energy costs, protracted quality issues, possible regulatory fines, and so forth.	• Devices inventoried and mechanism to prevent unauthorized devices from being connected to process networks • Redundancy at least at the distribution layer of networks, OSI layer 3 management of industrial network to process areas • Control programs maintained on a centralized system or equivalent • Additional protection such as badge readers, cameras, and so forth, to prevent unauthorized access and to allow for incident analysis and event correlation • Backup and recovery plans and incident response plans for security events • Controllers have cold spares available prestaged in process areas to ensure rapid process restoration, and so forth • SIS utilized in accordance with SIL requirements and some excess to accommodate from additional threats • Policies and training in line with industrial threats
4	• Catastrophic failures, irrecoverable process loss, long-term damage to reputation, irrecoverable or long-term recovery, massive product recalls, and so forth.	• Full redundancy on network • Full redundancy on control architecture in either hot spares or full online solution • All user actions tracked and monitored • Extensive use of SIS in excess of SIL requirements • Extensive policy, procedure, training, and so forth

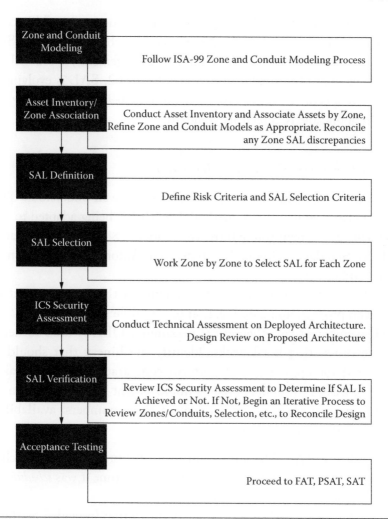

Figure 4.2 SAL workflow.

done: a target SAL for the ICS assets within scope, and a more audit-like assessment to determine the actual SAL profile of the ICS assets. The difference between the target and the actual profile can then be directly applied as aggregate vulnerabilities against which to assess risks, for given threats.

Future of SAL

The future of SAL is linked to the future of ISA-99, Part 2, which provides more specific guidance about controls and safeguards in ICS that can be used as a basis against which to determine SAL compliance. Much in the way audit standards such as SAS70 or ISEA (International Standard on Assurance Engagements) 3402 will be done against ITS standards such as ISO 27002, SAL is evolving as an ICS-specific auditing process against ISA-99, or potentially any other applicable ICS security standard.

Overall Equipment Effectiveness (Assessment)

Overall equipment effectiveness (OEE) is a well-understood quality control manufacturing methodology that is being adapted to ICS security assessment through the International Society of Automation (ISA) Standards Group 99—Industrial Automation and Control System Security.

OEE is a measurement of the maximum theoretical output for a given process, and a delineation of causal factors that prevent the achievement of this theoretical maximum. OEE is used to determine production bottlenecks, identify machinery that should be targeted for upgrades, and perform comparative analysis against like processes to support process improvement initiatives. The basic OEE measurement is the product of three numbers: availability, performance, and quality.

- *Availability*—Measure of uptime of the process—how much time was it actually up versus how much time it was *scheduled* to be up.
- *Performance*—Theoretical maximum output (provided by the equipment supplier or design engineer) for a machine or a line, say 1,200 cases per hour, and the actual throughput during the production window.
- *Quality*—How much was produced that was first-pass acceptable (no reworks, rejects, etc., that drag down OEE).

As an example, given the following,

MEASURE	VALUE
Availability	90%
Performance	95%
Quality	99.9%

the resulting OEE is (90/100) * (95/100) * (99.9)/100 or (90 * 95 * 99.9)/10,000, which is 85.4%.[13]

Determining what is acceptable, OEE is largely dependent on corporate culture and other practices, such as Six Sigma. Most organizations begin with a period of measurement first, then comparison across sites, and then systematic improvement. One very commonly known value once OEE is firmly established as a key performance indicator (KPI) is the per point increase or decrease in OEE, which means that any factors that clearly impact OEE can be associated easily for cost-benefit purposes.

Security OEE

Since OEE is intended to measure the theoretical versus real performance of a given process in terms of operational security, security OEE should try and determine how secure a system or process is in terms of deviation from the ideal security, which would translate to clearly meeting regulatory requirements, or industry standards, whether they be ISA-99 or NERC-CIP, CFAT, ISO, or internally developed security policy.

Therefore, a security OEE reading will tell managers how effective their spending on ICS security is at obtaining a fully compliant security posture in a language that they already understand. OEE also provides a means of measuring and tracking performance in security over time through quantitative metrics and repeatable measurements.

For security OEE, up-front effort must be taken to identify quantitative metrics representing availability, performance, and quality in a security context. Remember that quantitative metrics are generally those that would be interpreted the same by different people, for instance, defined measureable units like seconds, number of specific events, degrees, dollars, and so forth. Qualitative metrics are less precise—though very useful—and could be interpreted differently by different people during both measurement and assessment.

With availability there are a few security OEE metrics that may be accessible to measure in a security context. In some cases it may be necessary (and appropriate) to generate composite metrics—meaning that measurements and associated metrics from different, critical process elements are converted to a common scale and combined somehow, for instance, averaged.

A large majority of vulnerabilities in ICS are rate dependent, meaning availability issues associated with network outage, delay, jitter, and loss.[14] From this basis it becomes a matter of measuring network characteristics from in-line elements (switches/routers/firewalls/proxies) impacting OEE, and comparing them against the theoretical ideal or design target for the network.

Some metrics associated with ICS devices (for example, PLC, RTU), which are associated with availability, include issues such as:

- Loading
- Malfunctions
- Hardware failures

OEE availability metrics might also be composed of ICS server and terminal availability measurements. For instance, on average, how much time do the ICS historians and HMIs spend out of service due to patching or upgrades?

Probably the clearest sort of OEE metric associated with availability would be the amount of production time lost due to the shutdowns associated with the ICS itself. For instance, a malfunction in the ICS requires that production stop until the ICS is functional again, or perhaps start-up is delayed because the ICS is not ready or requires an inordinate amount of time to become fully functional after a restart. Production slowdown associated with ICS degradation is a performance metric. Production defects associated with ICS degradation are a quality metric. Keep reading.

With performance there are a few OEE metrics that may be accessible for measuring it in a security context. In some case it may be necessary (and appropriate) to generate composite metrics—meaning that measurements and associated metrics from different, critical process elements are converted to a common scale and combined somehow, for instance, averaged.

Measurements and metrics associated with adherence to ICS regulatory and security policy and operational procedures would be useful because they relate directly to manage resources required to effect remediation—or the level of risk that management is accepting—willingly or otherwise. For instance, suppose an audit reveals that security procedures overall are being followed only 50% of the time. While policy and procedural gaps may go unaddressed without impacting production, these gaps clearly elevate risk and therefore decrease the effective performance of the ICS security programs as a whole, whose role it is to reduce risk!

As with the availability metrics, the clearest sort of OEE metric associated with performance would be the amount of production decreases below maximum due to the production line slowdowns associated with the ICS. For instance, a malfunction in the ICS requires that product slow down until the ICS is fully functional again, or perhaps start-up is delayed because the ICS is not ready or requires an inordinate amount of time to become fully functional after a restart. However, production defects associated with ICS degradation are a quality metric. Keep reading.

Quality is a measure of the defect rate within a system. In this case the defects we are trying to understand are those within the ICS from a security context. Here are a few security OEE metrics that may be used to measure quality in a security context. In some cases it may be necessary (and appropriate) to generate composite metrics—again, meaning that measurements and associated metrics from different, critical process elements are converted to a common scale and combined.

The following are some measureable events or elements of the ICS that could be considered defects:

- Number of overprovisioned, defunct, or unidentifiable accounts within the ICS access control systems—physical and logical access controls alike. The ideal would be zero and the error rate would be the percentage of non-policy-compliant accounts within the entire population. For instance, if 25 accounts out of 100 are overprovisioned, defunct, or of unknown origin, then the error rate would be 25%.
- Proportion of ICS logs retained and accessible versus the target quality of logs under regulation or internal policy. For instance, suppose 3 years of historian data should be available, but in reality just 2 years can be recovered and retrieved, which equates to an error rate of 33%.

- If network IDS is in place, the proportion of events detected during deliberate scanning and probing (on a test network) by the IDS. For instance, if the IDS missed two out of five probes, there is an error rate of 40%.
- Number of documented and managed ICS network entry points versus the number of network entries discovered through a security audit. For instance, there are supposed to be 5 modems and 1 network gateway, but 10 modems were found and 1 wireless access point supporting a complete 254 IPv4 subnet address: Is this a high error rate?
- The error and loss rate on networks due to factors such as electromagnetic interference, long cable runs, damaged cables, and unauthorized traffic (a security metric in its own right).

Probably the clearest sort of OEE metric associated with quality would be the amount of production time lost due to the errors introduced by the ICS itself. For instance, a malfunction in the ICS requires that units of production be rejected because their quality is indeterminate.

Putting OEE Metrics Together

The final component of the OEE assessment is correlation to process efficiency measurement events discussed earlier: availability, performance, and quality. This measurement is accomplished through a variety of rules-based engines where data mining techniques are utilized to correlate the rate of occurrence of network events and process efficiencies—with the subsequent opportunity to measure improvement of process trends (and productivity and therefore profit potential) against network events.

To this point in our discussion, the OEE methodology largely does *not* distinguish between security events and anomalous or unintentional events known to cause process degradation or failures. However, the link between ICS security and profitability is established in a concrete manner through this OEE methodology, which increasingly serves the dual purpose of improved performance efficiency and improved security.

Further, not every organization uses OEE, though many companies consider it once they realize the full potential for continuous monitoring of process improvement initiatives. In the case where OEE is not used, commonly there are similar complex calculated key performance indicators (KPIs) (multiple spot measurements and formulas to compare values) that are of use. Some additional complex calculated KPIs include various yield, condition-based monitoring, power and energy management, and planned versus unplanned maintenance calculations.

Network-Centric Assessment

Rather than looking for vulnerabilities in ICS applications or devices on the network itself, network-centric risk assessment is about looking for illicit communications over benign or legitimate channels. This is easier said than done.

Network-centric analysis is relevant to ICS security because it provides the ability to flag suspicious activity regardless of whether a given device vulnerability is known or unknown.[15] Network-centric analysis is founded on the correlation of traffic patterns with intelligence lists of known or highly suspect sources and destinations on the Internet, versus signatures or anomalies. For instance, the Internet is full of infected or compromised devices and their associated IP addresses or even entire networks can be identified. Traffic to and from these places must be treated with utmost caution, but the addresses constantly shift and lists of such intelligence form the basis of network-centric intelligence.

Network-centric assessment and analysis starts with the observation of large traffic flows at the carrier level or by major security vendors to compile these intelligence lists of "devices behaving badly": devices engaging in attacks, spamming, hosting command and control systems for botnet and malware, and a wide variety of other telltale signs of malicious entities.

This type of risk analysis is not limited in its applicability to ICS and is not engineered specifically for ICS security purposes; however, it is particularly well suited to ICS security support because of its sensitivity to zero-day incidents that are not rate or signature dependent. In other words, network-centric assessment does not require the organizational assets to become infected or even degrade before risk can be assessed. Traffic from sources that would otherwise appear

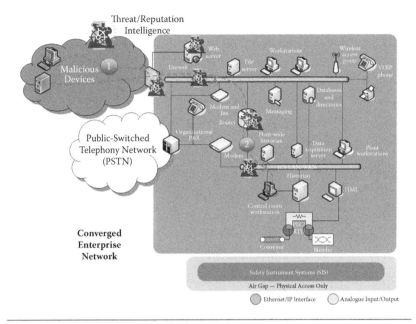

Figure 4.3 Converged enterprise network.

benign and are allowed to communicate with the network (whether a firewall, e-mail server, or Virtual Private Network (VPN) gateway for contractors) would be logged, reported, and blocked. For instance, if a maintenance contractor was working from a machine that has been observed participating in a botnet, but was otherwise functional for the unaware owner, its communications with the organizational system may trigger risk alerts and support real-time and proactive risk management. Alternately, if an infected machine was placed on the ICS network, the moment it tried to report its position to a "master" it could be detected before attack instructions arrive.

Figure 4.3 shows a form of a network-centric risk assessment architecture. In this design, critical network elements are seeded with intelligence related to known, bad IP addresses and domains on the Internet. When traffic from these sites arrives at the network perimeter, it is blocked regardless of the apparently benign nature of the connection. Similarly, when devices inside the ICS network attempt to connect to addresses on the banned list (even if they have no route from the ICS network), an alert is issued.

Network-Centric Compromise Indicators

Assessing Threat Agents, Force, and Velocity

In some cases, lists of known bad IP addresses and domains may not be available for use in seeding perimeter and internal network elements. In this case, network-centric analysis can also allow for the quantitative assessment of the IP addresses and geo-locations from which ICS assets are being probed randomly across a wide range of networks. The rate, force, and velocity of traffic from bad sources, whether it penetrates or not, is an excellent indicator of current risk. This approach requires the cooperation of a service provider or carrier.

Most, if not all, large carrier and service provider networks will employ systems for monitoring *traffic flows* through the major network junction points, both internally and at borders with other providers. A typical means of doing this is through the use of a proprietary but widely supported protocol from Cisco called Netflow or IPFIX.[16] Netflow allows providers to maintain a picture of traffic flows and volumes: basic tools for managing network quality and assurance. Netflow contains information about the traffic passing through network elements such as routers, which are the primary sources of Netflow. This information is useful for understanding the threats posed by entities using the network for illicit and malicious purposes. Basic information supported by Netflow includes source IP address, destination IP address, source port, destination port, ingress interface to the network, and some information about the type or quality of service associated with the traffic. Netflow does not capture packets or payloads, and is not a content/media interception technology.

Analysis on large carrier traffic flow statistics (via Netflow) is like a satellite view of road conditions—taking in an entire region or country at once, and with the ability to zoom down to very granular activities. Traffic flows can reveal the level of inbound threat from the Internet to an organizational device, or they can reveal internal devices "talking" over the Internet to suspicious external destinations.

From the perspective of the ICS network (connected to the corporate network, the Internet), there are two technical indicators associated with ICS assets that indicate poor security practices at best and compromise at worst.

Table 4.5 ICS Protocols and Ports

PROTOCOL	UDP PORT	TCP PORT
DNP3	ESP (IPSec) 20000	ESP (IPSec) 20000
Modbus		502
Ethernet/IP	2222	44818/2222
ICCP		102
OPC (TLS)	4840 (4843)	4840 (4843)
Profinet	34962/34963/34964	34962/34963/34964

Source: TCP/IP Port Numbers (TCP and UDP)—Network Services (IANA), http://www.honeypots.net/misc/services.

The first indicator is associated with *persistent traffic* flows over the Internet using protocols and ports that are idiosyncratic to ICS assets. For instance, Netflow analysis may reveal that a User Datagram Protocol (UDP) connection on port 20000 (a common ICS port; see Table 4.5) appears to have been established. Next, doing reverse name lookups (mapping the IP number to a domain name) on the destination IP may reveal what appears to be an ambiguous but likely inappropriate destination for ICS traffic, such as an ISP in China. Alternately, the destination may be a legitimate business, which happens to be a service provider to ICS users. In the former case (destination China), the indication would be that a compromise has occurred. In the latter case (destination service provider), the indication would merely be poor security architecture, which allows observable and identifiable ICS traffic over public networks.

Based on the use of Netflow analytics, it is possible to observe large amounts of scanning traffic, and the scans directed at ICS type protocols can be specially assessed. For instance, ICS devices are largely idiosyncratic in their use of the ports shown in Table 4.5.

Setting filters on Netflow analytics looking for packets directed at these ports can be a useful indication of which threat agents are deliberately targeting ICS devices that are on the open Internet. For instance, research of this nature published by Team Cymru in 2009 indicated that approximately 89% of such ICS asset scans observed appeared to come from IPs located in China.[17] However, it should also be noted that in the age of zombie botnets, the person that owns an asset seen scanning cannot be assumed to be guilty of any intent; their machine might be compromised!

The second compromise indicator for ICS assets that can be gathered from network-centric assessment is related to darkspace traffic originating from ICS user organizations. Darkspace is unassigned but routable and legitimate IP address space. Darkspace analysis is a sophisticated and increasingly employed means of detecting compromised devices either directly on the Internet or within organizations with gateways on the Internet. These compromised devices—frequently due to zero-day vulnerabilities, which have no antivirus signatures—will initiate scans looking for other devices to compromise and will inadvertently send probing packets into darkspace. By definition, any device entering darkspace is there either accidentally or for illicit purposes, such as sweeping for targets. To the extent that darkspace traffic is detected within or exiting from an ICS user organization, the presence of IT-based malware should be suspected. The greater the likelihood of IT-based malware, the greater the assessed risk to ICS as per our discussion in Chapter 2 about threats, where one of the most significant threats to ICS is not necessarily targeted attacks but collateral damage caused by malware scanning or consuming network resources. Darkspace analysis can also be done with enterprise networks, if network flow tools are available.

Other Network Infrastructure That Can Be Used for Network-Centric Analysis and ICS Security

Domain Name Server (DNS) infrastructure is known to be a critical asset worthy of direct attack because compromise of DNS services can result in wholesale compromise of dependent users.[18] Because malware command and control (C&C) servers rely on DNS to direct compromised devices "home," DNS services generate at least two useful pieces of information: who has been compromised by malware and who is launching attacks against specific assets.[19] It is very typical of the worst forms of malware to encode a DNS name as the call-home C&C address once a device has been compromised. Using a DNS name rather than an IP address provides the bot master the advantage of being able to change C&C servers to avoid detection and for redundancy. Awareness of the DNS names being used for C&C operations allows DNS administrators or security staff to set alerts whenever the malware domain is queried, and commence response operations since the device is very likely compromised or at best fatally curious. A second useful factor generated by DNS intelligence is heuristics of the malware (port, protocol, payload sizes, communications frequency, and timing). Because successful malware is so often zero day and no signatures exist from the IDS/intrusion prevention systems (IPS)/anti-virus (AV) vendors, these heuristics provide enough information to trace compromised machines on the internal enterprise network without the benefit of the binary signatures.

Messaging analysis and associate e-mail infrastructure are *de rigueur* for coping with the fact that 95%+ of e-mail on the Internet is illicit. A significant by-product of large-scale message cleaning is the security insight available from messaging patterns associated with ICS user organizations. Message cleaning consists of inbound and outbound message filtering. Inbound filtering is related to messages arriving at the messaging aggregation point from external domains. Inbound filtering metrics indicate the type and relative scale threats to the ICS user organization when compared to scale metrics from the Internet as a whole and other specific, non-ICS industries. Outbound filtering is related to messages leaving an organization for external domains. Reports from outbound filters are of particular interest because they can indicate security issues related to data leakage, inappropriate usage, misconfigurations, and especially devices compromised by known threats/malware that in turn can impact ICS.

Peer-to-peer (P2P) analysis, also known as traffic shaping, is another key element for potentially detecting threats to ICS user organizations. P2P analysis involves real-time inspection of traffic streams from ICS user gateways and domains looking for telltale signs of file sharing applications such as Kazaa, eMule, bitTorrent, and a range of other similar tools. These applications will distinguish themselves not just by large bandwidth consumption, but also by the ports and protocols they use, the nature of the payload, and the destinations they may be communicating with in order to coordinate file sharing. P2P channels are also frequently employed by malware for C&C and information exfiltration.

P2P infrastructure can be configured to monitor and issue alerts when new P2P sessions are initiated from ICS user domains, which should absolutely not have P2P traffic. For instance, P2P traffic exiting from most enterprises is an indication of misuse of corporate network assets at best, and malware compromise at worse. It is also a well-established fact that many P2P applications will be dual purpose: they will support file sharing according to user expectations, but will also index and surreptitiously expose everything on the computer and connected network drives, including ICS topologies. For this last reason, no devices such as laptops with P2P software should be allowed to attach to ICS networks.

Network-Centric Assessment Caveats

There are several challenges to performing network-centric analysis on ICS networks. First, metrics about network traffic flows beyond the organizational perimeter up into the carrier or service provider core network greatly facilitate the assessment process; however, access to such information is not common and must be specially requested from the service providers. Alternately, vendors such as McAfee, Cisco, and Arbor all offer "intelligence feeds" about known bad IPs and domains on a global basis, but these are subscription services and require that you purchase their infrastructure solutions. Next, on the internal organizational network, gathering traffic flow metrics is a logically expensive process—it burdens the routers. Traffic flow metrics in a typical environment gathered for operations may only sample packets at rates of anywhere from 1:100 to 10,000:1. This provides sufficient information for network management but can also result in lost or incomplete intelligence. Capturing traffic flow metrics on a 1:1 basis (info about every packet) is not practical from a purely operational perspective. Similarly, large-scale logging of messaging, DNS requirements, and P2P traffic management statistics deviates from standard management procedures (where logs are typically basic and not tuned for security assessment purposes) and represents a resource-intensive requirement.

No single source of network-centric analysis (traffic flow, DNS, messaging, P2P) will catch all malware threats to ICS assets. Network-centric analysis is greatly enhanced by correlation of observations from the mentioned sources, where "blind spots" associated with the practical limits of deployment can be mitigated. The more correlation that exists among the sources for a given ICS network, gateway, address range, or autonomous system (ASN), the greater the probability of detecting threats or compromises of ICS assets or understanding the degree of threats ranged against those assets.

Conclusion

In the course of this chapter we have taken the reader through 12 different forms of risk assessment aimed at or adopted to ICS security. Of these systems, we considered the first eight to be well known and largely derivatives of well-understood qualitative risk assessment processes. In other words, risk assessment processes tend to rely upon measurements and metrics that might be different from one assessor to another, and therefore are more prone to inconsistent results. These qualitative systems for ICS risk assessment have the benefit of tradition and ease of use behind them. This is a substantial benefit because well-understood risk assessment processes have many practitioners available, and therefore are more likely to get performed: any risk assessment on ICS is generally better than no risk assessment. However, aside from inconsistency, traditional, qualitative assessment suffers from being frequently unsuccessful in justifying investment in ICS security. Why this is so is probably a combination of factors, but, above all, the qualitative nature of many traditional risks assessments is apparent to executives: the results are therefore suspect to people used to dealing with the accuracy of financial metrics, for instance. As a result, investments in inconclusively proven risks are themselves halfhearted and inconclusive themselves.

The last four ICS risk assessment techniques we identified as evolving, and they consumed about three-quarters of this chapter. These processes are all less than 4 years old and have been employed only a handful of times each. In some cases they are better documented in this chapter than anywhere else. So why have we chosen to focus so much time on these arguably immature risk assessment methodologies? Because they are the first generation of quantitative assessments relying on discrete metrics and measurements that can not only be repeated and duplicated by different practitioners, but also eventually be *automated*. Automation of risk assessment is the future of risk assessment. As threats emerge at faster and faster rates, and ICS infrastructures themselves become more automated, so too must many of the risk assessment processes. Identifying quantitative metrics upon which to repeatably and automatically assess ICS threats and rapidly (if not automatically) adjust mitigating controls will be the only way to manage risk in the future. Finally, the last four ICS risk assessment processes represent a large step toward assessment methodologies that provide quantitative evidence of threat, and clear metrics upon which to base return on investment (ROI) calculations and business case development. In the presence of such facts and figures, not unlike the financial spreadsheets they deal with all day long, executives are slightly less able to ignore evidence from security staff without accepting personal risks associated with liability and negligence.

Endnotes

1. North American Energy Reliability Council (NERC) Web site FAQ, http://www.nerc.com/page.php?cid=1|7|114.
2. *NERC Security Guidelines for the Electricity Sector: Vulnerability and Risk Assessment*, http://www.esisac.net/publicdocs/Guides/V1-VulnerabilityAssessment.pdf.
3. National Institute of Standards and Technology (NIST) 800-53v3: *Recommended Security Controls for Federal Systems*, Appendix I, p. 1-8, control CA-2.
4. Department of Homeland Security CCSP, http://www.us-cert.gov/control_systems/.
5. http://www.inl.gov/scada.
6. INL/EXT-05-02585 revision 1, *Control Systems Risk Decision Methodology*, Idaho National Laboratory report prepared for U.S. Department of Homeland Security, March 23, 2005.
7. Wayne Boyer and Mike McQueen, *Ideal Based Security Technical Metrics for Control Systems*, INL, Department of Homeland Security, 2007.
8. Department of Homeland Security CCSP CSET, http://www.us-cert.gov/control_systems/satool.html.
9. Dr. Nate Kube and Bryan Singer, *Security Assurance Levels: A SIL Approach to Security*, 2008.
10. James Gilsinn and Ragnar Schierholz, Security Assurance Level Vector, White Paper, 2010.
11. Ibid.
12. http://www.oee.com.
13. Bryan Singer, *Correlating Risk Events and Process Trends to Improve Reliability*, SCADA Security Scientific Symposiums, January 2010.
14. As evidenced in the Stuxnet attacks of 2010, any specific malware attack will possibly be highly specialized to the ICS equipment and less likely to be mitigated by a signature-based security system.
15. http://www.cisco.com/en/US/technologies/tk648/tk362/technologies_white_paper09186a00800a3db9.pdf.

16. Team Cymru, Who Is Looking for Your SCADA Infrastructure? 2009, http://www.team-cymru.org/ReadingRoom/Whitepapers/2009/scada.pdf.

17. Nominum, Layered Defenses to Prevent DNS Cache Poisoning, White Paper, 2009, http://www.nominum.com/.

18. At the highest level, there are two distinct variants of threat: threat-from and threat-to. Threat-from is about the threat agent and the resources and characteristics of a given agent. At the coarsest level, some threat-from information is free and widely available from sources like CERT, McAfee, Symantec, Counterpane, and plenty of others. These sources may provide the information about some of the agents currently active in the world, for instance, the country that is the apparent source of the most attacks, or types of organizations or individuals launching attacks (attempting to exploit exposures such as the virus of the day, worm of the day, phish of the day, software vulnerability of the day, patch of the day, and general bogey man of the day). This type of public domain threat-from information is of limited value because it does not contain specifically actionable intelligence. Ideally, threat-from information will contain detailed metrics such as apparent country (and network in the case of logical threats) of origin, organization of origin, estimated resources available to the agent such as money, skills, and time, motivation of the agent, and objectives of the agent. This sort of threat-from information is strategic in nature, not tactical: it will provide intelligence about the likelihood of success, and the expected force, velocity, and duration of exploitation attempts. Threat-to is asset specific. Like threat-from information, coarse threat-to information is also publicly available from sources such as the Department of Homeland Security/Public Safety Canada, Information Sharing and Analysis Centers (ISACs), and a variety of other open sources. These sources may provide information about which industries or sectors appear to be experiencing exploitations other than those previously observed. For instance, some of the most granular information related to publicly available threat-to is about financial losses year over year. Again, this type of public domain threat-to information is of limited value because it does not contain specifically actionable intelligence. Ideally, threat-to information will contain detailed metrics such as asset ownership, asset names and locations (physical and logical), asset role, asset interdependencies, asset valuation, and business impact assessments. This sort of threat-to information is rare, never in the public domain, and highly sought after by industry; it is highly tactical and can support detailed response and remediation, especially when combined with detailed threat-from information. Good insight from threat-to metrics will provide intelligence about the potential level of impact.

19. Lili Shue, *Peer-to-Peer Networking Security and Controls*, IT Governance Institute, 2003, http://www.enhyper.com/content/p2psecandcontrol.pdf.

5

WHAT IS NEXT IN
ICS SECURITY?

This chapter considers some major trends in technology that will shape and dramatically expand the discipline of ICS security in the coming years, particularly the advent of Internet protocol version 6 in combination with technologies allowing for the massive, widespread deployment of remote control devices and sensors.

The Internet of Things

The Internet of Things (IOT) is a term describing the uniquely identifiable devices and objects that include far more than merely computing devices, such as desktops, laptops, and servers. The IOT includes the new generation of smart phones with computing power comparable to some laptops, and the ability to penetrate both consumer and business markets at the same time. IOT includes ICS devices, as this book has discussed in detail and at length. The IOT includes radio-frequency identification (RFID)-embedded devices such as shipping containers, soda bottles, clothing, and even perishable food and consumable medicines. The IOT includes roads and highways, where sensors track congestions, climatic conditions, and even the distance between vehicles. The IOT includes sensors in railway lines that tell controllers where the trains are, and sensors in runways and airplanes that allow planes to land with even greater precision and safety. The IOT includes the light switches in homes and office buildings such that they can be remotely controlled, and within thermostats so that smart grid applications allow for energy conservation. The IOT includes disposable, temporary sensors deployed by law enforcement, military, and security firms to detect movement in restricted areas or people that are under surveillance. The IOT includes pets and agricultural stock. The IOT includes wild and endangered animals. The IOT will, in all likelihood include people, both law abiding and otherwise.

ICS and especially security are intrinsic in the IOT. Many, if not a vast majority, of the devices in the IOT are in fact control and sensing devices, versus computing or control interfaces used by humans. Therefore, it is fair to say that the IOT is the future of ICS, and ICS is the future of human development.

IPv6

There Is a New Internet Protocol in Town

The Internet is facing a major evolution, where IT equipment everywhere will require upgrading to handle the new protocol. It is almost upon us because in February 2011 we ran out of Internet protocol (IP) version 4 addresses for dispensation to regional Internet registries. When these regional Internet registries have dispensed their last IP addresses, there will simply be no Internet v4 addresses left, and any new organization or device/man/woman/child that needs an IP address will have to get a v6 address. Regional registries are forecast to run out of addresses themselves at different rates, with the Asian and North American registries exhausting supplies in late 2011 and 2012. African and Latin American registries are projected (at the time of this writing—second quarter of 2011) to have sufficient addresses through 2015 and beyond, but based on past projections around address exhaustion, this could be an overly optimistic forecast for Africa and Latin America. The meaning for us all is that most of the new devices pouring onto IP, such as mobile phones and remote ICS devices (under the IoT definition discussed above), will soon be compelled to start using v6. Security systems and practitioners must be ready.

In Brief: What Is IPv6?

IPv6 is the successor to the version of Internet number assignments (addresses) that has supported the global Internet to date, which was called IPv4. (IPv5 was an experiment in a multicast technology that was not intended to replace v4, as v6 is intended to do.) IPv4 is the numbering system that all of the Internet currently uses, and a vast majority of internal enterprise networks also use a portion of v4 known as private addressing, reserved within the IPv4 specification for this purpose.

IPv6 differs from IPv4 in a number of ways. IPv6 comes with the capability of supporting addresses 128 bits in length, using base-16 numbering. IPv4 supports only 32-bit address lengths and employs a base-10 numbering system. The result is that IPv4 has a maximum of approximately 4.3 billion addresses. IPv6 supports a trillion trillion trillion times that amount. When IPv4 was specified back in the early 1980s, it was thought that 4.3 billion was more than we could possibly need. But at that time it was also envisioned that only super computers would need IP addresses and desktop computing was still very expensive. No one foresaw not only cheap desktops and laptops, but phones, industrial sensors and controls, household appliances, and even light sockets all needing IP addresses.

Therefore the main benefit of IPv6 is virtually unlimited IP addresses for the coming Internet of Things.

What Does IPv6 Mean for My Business in General?

In theory, IPv6 will change things for the better: it is more efficient to manage, faster, makes it easier to grow and expand networks, has enhanced functions for communicating with many parties at once, and has native support for enhanced security.

More practically, it means work and risk, and for ICS users, probably more risk than for "all IT" firms without ICS assets. IPv6 is coming fast and is not an option. Those that delay their planning because they cannot yet "see" an internal need will eventually find themselves isolated in vestigial pockets of IPv4 users. Their online resources will become more difficult to access and their security tools will become less and less interoperable, and perhaps even inoperable in a hybrid world of internal v4 and external v6.

In the short to medium term, IPv6 means work because the move is complex. Internal networks will need to be entirely redesigned to support a vastly larger address space, and certain types of functionality like direct point-to-point routing and self-addressing will need to be monitored and controlled. From a security perspective, many functions are not necessarily new in IPv6, because they existed in a variety of manually exploitable fashions in IPv4. But under IPv6 they can be automated and executed by benign applications that are poorly configured, and generate massive security holes.

For larger organizations and especially organizations running ICS, converting networks will be a multiyear process that involves a "dual-stack" transition strategy requiring businesses to remain connected to both IPv4 and IPv6 networks until most of the Internet gets to "the other side." This is a process that is forecasted to take 5 years or more. In the case of ICS networks amortizing over the next one or two decades, the IPv6 strategy must be to support dual technologies for potentially a long time to come. Unfortunately, there are some things about IPv6 and its deployment that might place ICS networks under even more pressure than IT networks to transition sooner rather than later.

What Does the Switch to IPv6 Mean for the Security of My ICS Network?

The most spoken of security benefit of IPv6 is generally that it comes fully enabled for IPSec encryption of payload information. IPSec can be used in different modes (some of which only provide authentication, not encryption), but it still requires key distribution mechanisms, which are the complex part of the security process, whether under IPv4 or IPv6. Other security improvements that you can expect to see in your network will be both operational and technical in nature. Operationally, easier route management and more address allocation features will reduce costs and increase efficiency. Technical capabilities such as mandatory support for multicast will speed the adoption and deployment of applications that facilitate collaboration among local and remote staff, partners, and client—all good things. IPv6 networks are also more flexible and easier to renumber and redesign according to evolving requirements related to applications or physical space. From an ICS perspective, IPv6 and the network elements that support it are generally more intended to support quality of service (QoS) and different sorts of service. Putting priority on ICS traffic, and even securely tunneling within it, becomes more viable as the network stack itself will accomplish these goals, rather than third-party or external application layers on top of the network stack.

The most spoken of security threat from IPv6 has to do with the transition to IPv6 from v4. The threat is that v6 traffic is pretty much jibberish to v4-only security devices and appliances, and can IPv4 be tunneled over v4 and used to evade established security. For instance, Ethernet (IEEE 802.3) is not different to IPv4 and IPv6; they will both gratefully use it as the layer 2 transport. Therefore a device that has both IPv4 and v6 network stacks can communicate over Ethernet using either or both types of IP. From a security perspective, if v4 is the well-engineered and secure layer 3 network, and v6 is basically unobserved, then malware and malicious entities will gravitate to v6 and attack hosts on the v6 interface. Since many operating systems support v6 natively now, this is a viable attack route for desktops and servers. From an ICS perspective, we only just got to IPv4 and now we are supposed to move? All the troubles that ICS devices experience with fragile network interfaces under v4 will possibly reemerge under v6; at the very least, we should assume that some mistakes will be repeated. But this assumes that the ICS network needs to go to v6 before it is amortized and evergreened. Is that a good assumption?

Let us look at some of the mechanics of IPv6 migration, and what is voluntary for organizations and what is compelled.

What Will the Move to IPv6 Require, for IT and ICS?

IPv6 brings operational and technical security benefits, but it will be a slow transition that involves building IPv6 capacity alongside existing IPv4. In practice, this will mean that networking devices that perform routing or switching and security elements (firewalls, intrusion, detection, etc.) will be first on the migration path.

Establishing an IPv6 lab is generally considered the first step in understanding the implications of v6 on an organizational infrastructure. At a minimum, a v6 lab will consist of the following devices operating in dual stack where possible (supporting both v4 and v6):

- v6-enabled endpoints such as programmable logic controllers (PLCs), remote terminal units (RTUs), laptops, desktops, and servers
- A v6 router
- A v6 switch

- A v6 firewall
- A v6 Domain Name Server (DNS)
- A v6 Dynamic Host Control Protocol (DHCP) server

Other things that would be recommended for a v6 lab, given the requirement for secure networks, may be:

- A v6-aware network intrusion detection system/prevention system (IDS/IPS)
- A v6-aware host-based firewall and intrusion detection to load on the test endpoints
- A v6 Network Time Protocol (NTP) server
- A v6-enabled directory server

Many ICS applications will gain their v6 ability from the operating system they are based upon; for instance, Windows. Often this capability will be introduced as a default feature or a patch or update, or is already present.

All ICS networks and their operators have a technical necessity to develop v6 skills, even if v6 networks are not on the internal technical road map for the ICS. The specific reason for this is that from 2011 onward the population of v6 devices will explode, and sooner or later they will interface with the v4 ICS networks. For instance, the following sorts of devices might be introduced into the ICS network on short notice:

- IPv6-enabled platforms that support ICS historians, human–machine interfaces (HMIs), and other control assets
- Dual-stack (v6-enabled) digital-to-analogue (DAC) converters that might sit in front of PLCs, RTU, etc.
- Address translation devices that might sit between ICS segments that must remain v4 (because upgrade to v6 is not possible on endpoint devices) and support v6.

ICS v6 Test Lab Designs

Establishing a v6 testing lab is the first step to managing risks associated with ICS and v6, even if there is no intention of using v6 directly in ICS. Labs provide information about the unknown world of v6 and ICS, and make risk management practical.

While it is frequently the case that ICS test labs are not available because they were not included in the original business case for the production system, v6 labs can be simple and cheap to stand up. It is also possible that carriers and service providers have established labs that can be borrowed or rented, as a means of encouraging migration of supporting risk management efforts.

Stage 1 Test Environment: Introduce IPv6

Test the effect of v6 devices on the same v4 virtual local area network (VLAN) as ICS devices. As illustrated in Figure 5.1, a v6-enabled OS such as a modern version of Windows Vista can be installed, and it will start to make the necessary v6 advertisements on the network looking for routers, DNS, and DHCP services as defined in the v6 specification. The impact of this v6 traffic can be difficult to predict perfectly, especially given that this traffic may in fact be "audible" by other devices that have v6 interfaces activated by default, but have had no other device to communicate with to date. Similarly, the v6 test device may be configured to inject certain sorts of rogue v6 messages, such as router announcements (RAs). While this might appear to introduce a more remote threat associated with a malicious threat, it should also be considered that RAs and similar v6 control messages could potentially be generated by careless administration, not only malicious intent.

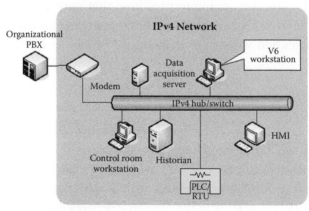

Stage 1 — v6 Device on v4 Test Network

Figure 5.1 Stage 1 v6 test lab.

Stage 2 — v6 Test Network

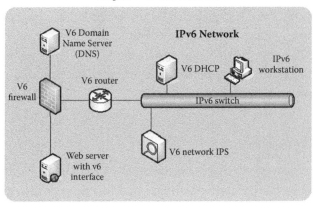

Figure 5.2 Stage 2 v6 test lab.

Stage 2 Test Environment: Sense IPv6

Establish a v6 test zone for v6-only devices as seen in Figure 5.2, and test intrusion detection of network analytics to sense IPv6. Even though there may be no intention of deploying a v6 network, it is operationally mandatory to understand how it works to assess and manage the v6 threats. For instance, the rapid advent of v6 malware makes the management of dual-stack security elements important to maintaining visibility of any network, even a nominally v4-only network. v6 malware must be detectable, because it will be introduced sooner or later, most likely from a device running v4 in what appears to be a perfectly "hygienic" manner. Elements such as v6 DNS and v6 DHCP are of more interest to those that must interface or support v6 devices; those without such requirements may wish to defer experimentation with these elements in the labs as appropriate.

Stage 3 Test Environment: Dual-Stack Testing

Establish an ICS zone a dual-stack network to assess operational loads and risks, see Figure 5.3. Dual-stack networks will become short-term requirements for ICS because wireless devices will increasingly be v6 and will transition from v6 networks through dual-stacked devices either on the network perimeter or in the enterprise network core. Also, it may be the case that remote devices (such as wireless) using off-the-shelf cellular

Stage 3 — Dual Stack Network

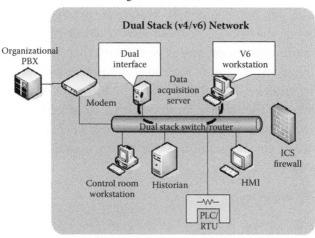

Figure 5.3   Stage 3 v6 test lab.

infrastructure will come with "native" v6 interfaces on the cellular radio and data connection from the carrier. Attempting to translate between v6 and v4 may be more effort than enabling a v6 interface on the acquisition server or historian. The effects of this additional interface may differ from theory to practice and require testing. Additionally, if the cellular carriers are translating v6 to v4 before placing the traffic on the open (v4) Internet, then security such as VPN communications may not function as expected. In these cases it may be that adopting private architectures, where IP is routed directly from remote cellular devices to company networks, is the solution. (See the below discussion on ICS and wireless.) But this solution may still require that the company be able to manage the v6 that comes directly from the device over the private architecture rather than through the Internet. Private architectures are available from many cellular carriers for data connections.

Stage 4 Test Environment

Stage 4 involves creating a tunnel of v6 communications through v4 ICS networks and see impacts on network elements and potentially any other devices on old-fashioned spans with hubs instead of switches. This would simulate a condition where a remote wireless device is coming from a v6 network with a v6 IP address directly into the ICS network, for instance, through a private architecture discussed above (see Figure 5.4). Testing at this stage should include the ability of network security devices to detect tunneled traffic. It is a common concern related to v6 security that v4 security devices such as firewalls, intrusion detection, and proxies will not recognize v6 traffic tunneled inside v4 packets, and allow it to pass through unrecognized. The danger in allowing v6 communications to tunnel without any detection or analysis is that a whole communications infrastructure can be established without any controls on it.

Stage 5 Test Environment

In Stage 5, we test NATing (network address translation) of v6 to v4 and vice versa. NATing is a critical element of understanding the impact of v6 on ICS devices. While we have made it the last stage of testing, it could easily be a higher priority in different organizations and occur sooner.

The advent of v6 devices and networks does not spell the end of v4 network and wholesale migration of devices to the new network. v4 will persist for many years to come. Dealing with the legacy of v4 will require capabilities related to NATing: the ability to translate network communications between v6 and v4 networks. There are several available solutions for NATing, but not of them is considered standard: it is a matter of what makes sense under given conditions and architectures and especially what the devices and operating systems themselves can support. Some v6-v4 NAT systems work by including the v4 address at the end of the v6 address; other systems completely obscure the v4 address from the v6 address—much like current generations of v4-only NAT, which function to conserve IP addresses rather than interoperability. But regardless of which addresses are incorporated, the greatest difficultly is that v4 and v6 differ substantially in the area of packet headers, which define important properties of the data within the payload. The diversity of v6 headers is not supported in v4, and communications passing through NATs could see important characteristics being stripped out or "lost in translation." For instance, the "type of service" field in v4 is not part of the v6 header, meaning quality of service flags are very different. These changes must be projected and accounted for by ICS engineers; otherwise, unpredictable behaviors

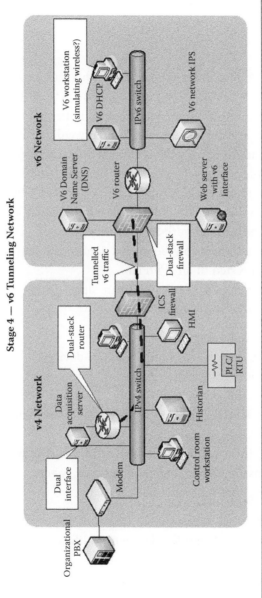

Figure 5.4 Stage 4 v6 test lab.

will certainly emerge. Another example, how does NATing impact the stateful security in proxies and VPNs used in remote administration by ICS maintenance staff and contractors/suppliers? See Figure 5.5 for an example of a NATing test design.

Dual Stacking

After an ICS v6 test lab, the next step on this path is to start to make internal network devices dual stack. A dual-stack device speaks both IPv4 and IPv6, and can route and manage both types of networks at the same time. Security equipment especially will need to be upgraded to dual stack at the same rate as the network elements because it is entirely possible that as soon as v6 is available, something bad will attempt to use it as a back channel to attack or remove information.

The move to dual-stack support may require either a software or a hardware upgrade to network and security elements. For this reason, the migration will probably be staged across different network segments, but first tested in an IPv6 lab.

Equipment that will require software upgrades or replacement to support dual v4/v6 stacks includes:

- Switches and routers and load balancers
- Endpoint devices (desktops, mobile devices, ICS elements like RTUs and PLCs)
- Network support infrastructure: Domain Name Services (DNS), DHCP, directory services, Network Time Protocol (NTP)
- Security infrastructure: firewalls, intrusion prevention and detections, analytics and data capture systems (since NAT addressing will no longer be required)

Much of this sort of equipment may be IPv6 capable with a software or firmware update if the device has sufficient storage and memory space for the new IPv6 stack. The obvious exception is devices used in ICS with their limited memory; however, ICS are not the only sorts of devices that may not transition so well to a v6 environment. IP assets such as cameras, building safety systems like intercoms, door strikes, smoke detectors, and other converged devices may find themselves in a difficult situation when faced with a v6 environment.

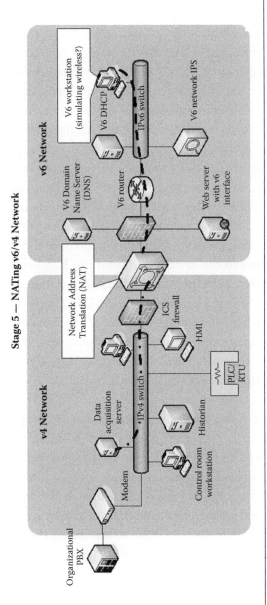

Figure 5.5   Stage 5 v6 test lab.

ICS and Cellular Wireless

One instance of particular interest to ICS is the advent of v6 on modern cellular wireless networks, which had already began in 2011. Carriers will rapidly be migrating handset and smart phones to a v6 environment because they simply do not have the necessary IP addresses to support these devices and they do not want to be faced with the longer-term management costs of running v4 internal devices addressing while the remainder of the Internet goes v6. More simply, why deploy a new infrastructure for high-speed wireless data using a legacy networking standard such as IPv4? Also, the cellular wireless business in many countries is competitive and cost-sensitive, and support for dual-stack technologies essentially makes a service provider less competitive, providing a driver for rapid and total migration to v6.

For most mobile devices, native support for v6 is already available on the handset operating system or in the radio firmware. Where this is not the case, carriers have the ability to do over-the-air provisioning: push patches to the devices. However, for ICS devices using cellular technologies, such in-field provisioning are (hopefully) disabled because of the potential impact on the devices and the processes they are monitoring. So what is to be done if the wireless network is going v6, but the endpoint devices have a fully integrated IPv4 broadband radio? And the risks associated with performing a significant change like replacing the network stack are unknown?

One answer is that the wireless ICS devices should be tested in a v6 test lab. Of course, this means that resources have to be applied to create a v6 test lab in the first place. An alternative to building a v6 test lab may be to rent time in an existing lab. For instance, most telecommunications carriers will have established several such labs for internal use and customer support. Inquiring about access to such labs with your service providers is a good option, just do not expect that they will be able to support testing of ICS devices or even have testing methodologies appropriate to ICS. But there is also the "private" architecture alternative.

Private Architecture and Cellular Wireless

Cellular (wireless) broadband has made tremendous strides in speed and coverage in the last few years. Between 2001 and 2011, the data speeds available through broadband cellular wireless to the Internet have increased by roughly 40 times (4,000%), and things will only get better. In 2001, CDMA 1xRTT and GSM were the dominant cellular data technologies with about 128 Kbps of throughput available under the right conditions. This was about as fast as a good modem in 1992, but useful nonetheless from an ICS perspective. Rather than pay to have fragile telephone lines extended to remote ICS locations, cellular data became a much simpler and more widely available technology. Whereas expensive technologies (relatively) like packet radio had certainly been supported by ICS wireless well before 2001, the dramatic reductions in cost and increases in coverage started to spur more wireless services into ICS infrastructures for remote devices.

Broadband wireless services use the Internet by default. It has always been this way and represents a learning curve for carriers because a whole new section of their infrastructure is suddenly exposed to new threat agents and vulnerabilities. In the early days of CDMA and GSM, it was not uncommon to find that the service providers lacked many security controls on the back-haul networks that connected the wireless devices to the Internet. This meant that the mobile devices enabled a completely open and routable IP address to the device or system they were providing connectivity to. If that device possessed any unpatched vulnerabilities, they could be exploited just like any desktop system connected to an Internet service provider. Additionally, because all data were routed over the Internet, it was subject to easier disruption, observation, and potentially interception. In 2001, running at modem speeds, wireless was widely used for was business applications, but was seeing adoption with ICS where availability threats might not have been considered high—and confidentiality threats may not even have been considered. Despite the hype, wireless data in early days generated inflated expectations and a few spectacular business failures: remember WAP (Wireless Access Protocol)? As a result of these factors—slow speed, limited adoption—the threat environment did not mature for lack of targets; many security lessons were never learned about broadband wireless. But broadband wireless has changed dramatically in the intervening years and hard, new security lessons will be learned if the old assumptions about threats and cellular wireless persist.

The new speeds available with modern broadband wireless like High-Speed Packet Access (HSPA) bring massive benefits in the form of new functionality and capability. For instance, it is entirely feasible to not only perform telework with these connections, but also do voice-over IP, video conferencing, run virtual terminal, and even support large file transfers! The advent of smart phones such as the iPhone, new generation of BlackBerry phones, and other competing products has also enriched the asset pool that is available through wireless: the targets on wireless data connections are more attractive because of the commercial and personal information they manage. As a result, targeting of wireless broadband networks by threat agents is now commonplace, and in fact undifferentiated from targeting of fixed-line broadband. This means that scans and probes are observable against wireless devices on a routine basis, and like the fixed-line Internet, insecure devices stand a substantial chance of being compromised. In the case of ICS devices and their known fragility, the mere act of scanning may be enough to impact performance. Cellular wireless is well past the 5 Mbps speed—so the force and velocity of attacks over a wireless interface is within the realm of direct Ethernet connections now.

Now that wireless broadband is just another form of Internet connection with all the same threats and risks, routing alternatives such as private architectures merit consideration.

A private architecture for broadband wireless allows traffic from remote ICS or other devices to be routed directly from the mobile carrier back-haul network to the organizational network without touching the Internet (see Figure 5.6). Mobile carriers associate the wireless devices with private architectures so that the IP packets from these devices are recognized as "not for the net" and are directed down private virtual connections within the carrier network directly to the organizational gateways. Technologies such as multiprotocol label switching (MPLS) are specifically intended to support this type of functionality and are found in the core of most modern carriers. Private architectures for ICS devices, whether v4 or v6, are considered a best practice and offer substantially reduced attack opportunities at what amounts to low cost: carriers will generally not charge a substantial monthly premium for private architecture. However, in order to get a private architecture, it may be required that the carrier be the provider of both the cellular and fixed-line network services for the organization.

Private Architecture

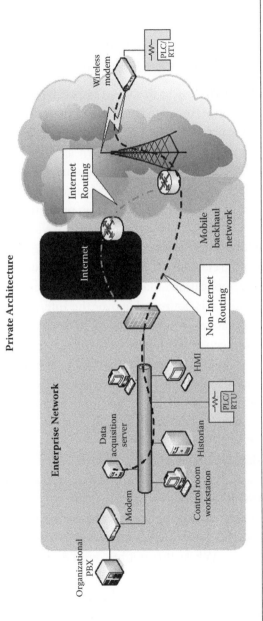

Figure 5.6 Private architecture for broadband wireless.

v6 Security Testing Methodology for ICS Devices

Security testing methodologies for v6 and ICS will not be remarkably different from v4, though a few important additions within v6 may certainly generate unpredictable conditions that should certainly be reviewed. The following are points of security differences between IPv4 and v6 to be aware of when testing.

- The ability for v6 devices to self-address can potentially allow devices to choose from huge address ranges. This is a benefit from the perspective of making devices more resilient to the failure of network infrastructure such as DHCP, but it has downsides too. For instance, not knowing the IP address of a remote field device that has decided to self-address could make identification and administration problematic. Controls associated with disabling or managing this v6 network stack feature within ICS devices and networks should be verified.
- Multicast is an element of IPv4 but not widely used until fairly recently for applications like voice and video conferencing or IPTV. Multicast is not routable over the Internet. As a result, multicast is probably never seen on ICS networks and only occasionally seen on corporate networks in recent years. But multicast is a mandatory and important part of v6 communications and management. ICS devices even in the proximity of a v6 network should be verified for tolerance of multicast traffic, because it is timely to appear on the network. In fact, one of the first things a v6 device will do when connected to a network is look for multicast support.
- Crypto capabilities are native to IPv6, and are one of the touted benefits to security associated with v6 migration: that point-to-point encryption with IPSec is a part of the specification, and third-party applications are no longer needed to support IPsec. While this might sound easy to apply, a new layer of security in practice, it is not as easy as to employ. Other forms of infrastructure like key management servers are needed, and therefore would require either new services to be available to the ICS network or new servers to be introduced into the ICS network. Furthermore, encryption is never free; it is computationally expensive for devices to perform. If

an ICS device supports a modern v6 network stack, it is still an entirely different matter as to whether or not it can support IPSec crypto and still function as intended. Load testing before and often IPsec enablement will absolutely be required.

- Jumbograms are substantially larger than typical payloads within v6 packets that are unfragmented. Jumbograms start at 65,536 bytes and get larger. Because of their potential size, jumbograms are known to present denial of service threats, as they can consume large amounts of network bandwidth and processing resources on routers and switches. In an ICS environment that supports v6 either through dual-stack elements or on a dedicated basis, the introduction of jumbograms in a perfectly legitimate manner under the v6 standard could cause severe latency. Similarly, even allowing devices on the ICS network to tunnel v6 over v4 means that if these tunneling devices happen to send or receive jumbograms, serious impacts could be felt on the ICS network resources. Finally, jumbograms employ distinct header flags that might result in a network stack failure on a device with a v6 stack that has not been adequately tested in advance.

- In v6, extensions to headers are common and widely used for a variety of intended v6 functions, such as point-to-point security, quality of service, and jumbograms. The result is that v6 possesses a wider range of header flag alternatives and header extension combinations from v4. The fuzzing and other sorts of randomized stack testing that was employed for v4 will need to not only be reperformed for v6, but enhanced. Testing a v6 device using the stack testing methodologies and tools developed for v4 stacks and devices is entirely insufficient.

- The need to translate network traffic from v6 remote devices to internal v4 networks will be commonplace—if for no other reason than much ICS infrastructure will see delayed upgrade to v6 for lack of current vendor support. The ability to maintain stateful communications when NATing from v6 to v4 and vice versa is not guaranteed, and in some instances may not be possible. The alternative to relying on stateful NATing is to engage in static port forward in the NAT device mediating between v6 and v4. There ICS security testing should consider the requirement to maintain state and test the technical solution that has the highest chance of success: stateful NATs and static port forwarding on NATs.

This is not an exhaustive list of security differences between IPv4 and IPv6, and their effect on security.

IPv6 and ICS Sensors

We started this chapter with an Internet of Things (IOT) discussion. Most IOT will be very simple devices operating in mesh—hence the requirement for something like an IPv6 network extension to low-power wireless personal area (small area) networks (LoWPANs)[1] to link simple device to the brains that correlate and aggregate data and make decisions.

LoWPAN is a simple low cost communication network that allows wireless connectivity in applications with limited power and relaxed throughput requirements. A LoWPAN typically includes devices that work together to connect the physical environment to real-world applications, e.g., wireless sensors. LoWPANs conform to the IEEE 802.15.4-2003 standard (IEEE802.15.4).

Some of the characteristics of LoWPANs are as follows:

1. Small packet size. Given that the maximum physical layer packet is 127 bytes, the resulting maximum frame size at the media access control layer is 102 octets. Link-layer security imposes further overhead, which in the maximum case (21 octets of overhead in the AES-CCM-128 case, versus 9 and 13 for AES-CCM-32 and AES-CCM-64, respectively), leaves 81 octets for data packets.
2. Support for both 16-bit short or IEEE 64-bit extended media access control addresses.
3. Low bandwidth. Data rates of 250 kbps, 40 kbps, and 20 kbps for each of the currently defined physical layers (2.4 GHz, 915 MHz, and 868 MHz, respectively).
4. Topologies include star and mesh operation.
5. Low power. Typically, some or all devices are battery operated.
6. Low cost. These devices are typically associated with sensors, switches, etc. This drives some of the other characteristics such

as low processing, low memory, etc. Numerical values for "low" elided on purpose since costs tend to change over time.

7. Large number of devices expected to be deployed during the lifetime of the technology. This number is expected to dwarf the number of deployed personal computers, for example.

8. Location of the devices is typically not predefined, as they tend to be deployed in an ad-hoc fashion. Furthermore, sometimes the location of these devices may not be easily accessible. Additionally, these devices may move to new locations.

9. Devices within LoWPANs tend to be unreliable due to variety of reasons: uncertain radio connectivity, battery drain, device lockups, physical tampering, etc.

10. In many environments, devices connected to a LoWPAN may sleep for long periods of time in order to conserve energy, and are unable to communicate during these sleep periods.[2]

Pros and Cons of IPv6 and Low-Power (Wireless) Devices

IPv6 possesses two primary characteristics that will drive LoWPANs toward it:

1. The ability to include autoconfiguration of both addresses and networks.
2. A massive address space capable of supporting trillions of unique devices.

However, IPv6 brings a variety of challenges, which stand in the path of the IOT vision and the integration of LoWPAN-based, ICS type devices in the larger control networks hosting the "brains of these many small devices." The brains are things such as historians and SCADA controllers for not just manufacturing systems, but air and surface traffic control, energy grids, agricultural sensors, geolocation information systems (GIS), RFID readers, and other assets. Some of these challenges may appear to be a restatement of the "why ICS is different than IT" debate that still continues, though in the context of futuristic networking technologies.

The first challenge is security. LoWPAN devices will be necessarily simple, and support only enough configuration and management capability to ensure functionality, not security. Indeed, while the advent of massively dispersed and integrated ICS type devices will have major safely benefits, it will invoke some pernicious security issues. If devices are intended to be as logically light as possible, building in firewalls and other security features may not be viable. Such ICS networks based on LoWPAN or similar layer 2 transports will need highly planned segregation and intrusion prevent technologies at the edge where they interface with more powerful devices relaying their traffic to aggregation and analysis tools. These larger tools will probably have larger power sources, and therefore support the security capabilities we generally associate with modern IP-enabled systems. As previously discussed, the prospect of ASIC-based security capabilities is a further area for development.

Under these conditions, LoWPANs managing ICS interactions on critical systems could become susceptible to a variety of (largely denial of service) attacks if traffic can be changed, removed, or injected:

- Flooding a low-bandwidth network could be a trivial undertaking.
- Injecting packets designed to confuse the ICS devices without the internal logic to reject or examine packets in anything but rudimentary manners.
- Injecting packets can force devices into sustained layer 2 backoff (they want to avoid wireless collisions of data and so wait indefinitely for "quiet").
- Injecting erroneous routing instructions can cause data to be lost or inflict DOS attacks on neighboring devices.
- Injecting forged packets can indicate false information and events from ICS devices, and cause operators to perform inappropriate actions.

The second challenge is interoperability. LoWPAN or any other small-device ICS protocols connecting meshes within meshes wirelessly will have to be as light as possible. The current LoWPAN is built to support packets of no more than 128 bytes, while IPv6 specifies a minimum packet size of 1280 octets. How to shoehorn an IPv6 packet into a layer 2 LoWPAN transport must be addressed, without consuming dramatically more power and bandwidth. For instance,

IETF sums up one critical issue of adopting IPv6 to future and ICS devices and protocols like this:

> Header Compression: Given that in the worst case the maximum size available for transmitting IP packets over an IEEE 802.15.4 frame is 81 octets, and that the IPv6 header is 40 octets long (without optional headers), this leaves only 41 octets for upper-layer protocols, like UDP and TCP. UDP uses 8 octets in the header and TCP uses 20 octets. This leaves 33 octets for data over UDP and 21 octets for data over TCP. Additionally, as pointed above, there is also a need for a fragmentation and reassembly layer, which will use even more octets leaving very few octets for data. Thus, if one were to use the protocols as is, it would lead to excessive fragmentation and reassembly, even when data packets are just 10s of octets long.[3]

To build on these challenging observations: encryption of data payloads will exacerbate this situation even further!

A Few Years Yet...

While the IOT and trillions of ICS-like sensor devices are very likely in our future as security practitioners, and bring new and ever tougher challenges, this scenario is definitely future focused and not in the here and now. These specifications we have touched on are still largely used in laboratories and proof-of-concept demonstrations rather than functional environments. Security issues and solutions such as these will be the make-or-break factors as we attempt to extend controls and sensors ever further into new domains and infrastructures by 2020 and beyond.

Endnotes

1. http://en.wikipedia.org/wiki/6LoWPAN.
2. http://tools.ietf.org/html/rfc4919.
3. Ibid., IETF RFC 4919.

Index

A

ActiveX controls, 72
Address Resolution Protocol
    (ARP), 75
Adobe, 63
Antivirus software, 65, 79; *See also*
    specific software
Aurora experiments, 111, 113
Automated banking machines
    (ABMs), 31

B

Bittorrent, 62
Blogs, 63
Blue-sky convergence, 31–32
Border Gateway Protocol (BGP), 35
Botnets, 59, 64–65, 68, 69, 70–71, 73,
    80, 156; *See also* Malware

C

Cellular wireless, 176–178
Chemical Facility Anti-Terrorism
    Standards, 4

Cisco, 159
Cisco Express Forwarding (CEF),
    75
Command and control (C&C)
    communications channels,
    70, 71, 73
Common criteria assessment, 143
Common Vulnerabilities and
    Exposures (CVE)
    database, 105
Computer Emergency Readiness
    Team (CERT), 18, 57
Computer Emergency Response
    Team, 3
Consequence matrices, 138–139
Continuity, business, 35–36
Control Systems Security Program
    (CSSP), 18, 135–136
ControlNet, 4
Convergence, network; *See*
    Network convergence
Counterpain, 57
Cyber Emergency Response
    Team, 135

D

DCOM technology117
De-Militarized Zone (DMZ)
    technology, 53
De-standardization, 37–38
Defense, Department of, 111
Denial of control (DoC), 109–110,
    114, 120
Denial of service (DOS), 119–120
Denial of view (DoV), 108, 112,
    114, 120
Device stack management, 145
DeviceNet, 4
Digital Subscriber Loop (DSL), 38
Disaster recovery, 35–36
Distributed control systems (DCS),
    4, 6, 18, 19, 20
Distributed denial of service
    (DDOS) attacks, 62, 120
Distributed Network Protocol-3
    (DNP3), 24
DNS attacks, 66, 67
Domain Name Server (DNS), 157–159

E

EDonkey, 62
Encryption, 88, 180
Energy, Department of, 136–137
Enterprise resource planning (ERP)
    systems, 64–65
Enterprise risk management
    (ERM), 99, 100
Espionage, industrial, 62
Ethernet, 24, 40, 167

F

Facebook, 63
Federal Energy Regulatory
    Commission (FERC), 5
Firewalls, 40, 50, 53, 65–66, 72,
    79, 131

Foreign intelligence agencies, 59
Frame Relay, 38
Fully qualified domain names
    (FQDNs), 70, 76
Fuzzing, 120–121, 133
Fuzzy logic optimization, 21

G

Geolocation information systems
    (GIS), 183
Gnutella, 62
Green network stacks, 116

H

Hi-jacked proxies, 76
Hi-jacking malware, 64–68, 69, 77;
    See also specific types
Homeland Security, Department
    of, 6, 18, 58, 126, 129–130
Human–machine interface (HMI),
    21–22, 90, 94
Hypertext Transport Protocol
    (HTTP), 70, 76

I

Idaho National Laboratory (INL),
    105, 130–131, 132, 139–140
Idaho National Labs
    Recommended Practices
    Commission, 18
IEEE 802.3 Ethernet, 17
IEEE Power Engineering Society
    Standards, 14
Illegal site hosting, 62
Industrial automation and control
    systems (IACS), 6
Industrial control system (ICS); *See
    also* Security, industrial
    control system (ICS)
  acceptance testing, 104
  analogue, 22

architectures, private, 178
assets, identifiable, 58
assurance requirements, 87–88
availability, 83, 85, 86
cellular wireless, relationship
    between, 176
confidentiality, 83, 85, 88
consolidation of market, 16
control devices, viewing as, 106
data at rest, 94–95
emergence of, 40–41
encryption, 88
evolution of, 15–16, 88
hydraulic controls, 22
I/O interface, 106–107, 112
information display, 7
infrastructure, 111, 118
integrity, 83, 85
IPv6; *see* IPv6
IT, interfaces with, 9, 46,
    114–115, 115–116
legacy protocols, 24
life cycle of, 16–17
modem usage, 41
percentage of, in IP-enabled
    devices, 17
safety instrumented systems,
    versus, 8
security; *See* Security, industrial
    control system (ICS)
standardization, 22, 24
term, origin of, 6
usage of, 7–8, 9
vendor protocols, 26
vulnerabilities, 43, 45–46, 93–94,
    98–99, 104, 105–106, 114;
    See also Security, industrial
    control system (ICS)
Information Sharing and Analysis
    Centers (ISACs), 58
Information technology (IT)
    acceptance testing, 104–105

availability, 83, 84, 86
confidentiality, 83, 84, 88
encryption, 88
industrial control system (ICS),
    interfaces with, 9, 46,
    114–115, 116
integrity, 83, 84
management controls, 103
risk events, reporting of, 103
security, versus industrial control
    system (ICS) security, 8,
    50, 53, 98–99
vulnerabilities, 82, 93–94
International Organization for
    Standardization (ISO)
    standards, 3
International Services Digital
    Network (ISDN), 38
International Society of
    Automation (ISA), 6
    Standard 99, 19
International Standard of
    Assurance Engagements,
    3402, 148
Internet of Things (IOT), 163–164,
    182, 185
Internet Protocol
    convergence; *See* Network
        convergence
    dominance of, 40
    IPv6; *See* IPv6
    spoofing of, 133
Internet Relay Chat (IRC),
    70–71
Internet, growth of, 25
Intrusion detection systems (IDS),
    66, 131
Intrusion prevention systems
    (IPS), 66
IPFIX, 155
IPv6
    advantages of, 183
    disadvantages of, 183

dual-stack networks, 170–171, 174
efficiency, 165
encryption, 180
ICS sensors and, 182–183
ICS usage and, 165–166
IPv4, *versus*, 165, 167
overview, 164–165
requirements, 167–168
route management, 166
security of, 166, 167, 180–182,
    183–184
test labs, 168–169, 170–172, 174
ISA-99, 147–148

K

Killer apps, 25

L

Linux, 114
Loss of control (LoC), 110,
    112–113, 114, 120
Loss of view (LoV), 108–109, 112,
    114, 120
Low-power wireless personal area
    (LoWANs), 182, 183–185

M

Malicious code, 17
Malware, 59, 60–61, 62, 64–68, 69
    network resources, consumption
        of, 114–115
    new devices, attacks on, 104
    reproductive cycle of, 72, 73–75
Man-in-the-middle (MITM) attack,
    94, 121–122, 132
Manipulation of control (MoC),
    110–111, 113, 114, 122
Manipulation of view (MoV), 109,
    113, 114
McAfee, 57, 159

Modbus, 4, 24, 41, 117
MS Messenger, 63
Multicasting, 180
MySpace, 63

N

National Institute of Standards
    and Technology (NIST),
    3, 6, 59
    800-53, 128, 129
    800-82, 46, 50, 100, 128
    ICS risk assessment guidelines,
        126, 128–129
National SCADA Test Bed Program
    (NSTB), 130–131, 132
Netflow, 155, 156
Network convergence
    blue-sky convergence, 31–32
    competitive drivers, 36–37
    cost drivers, 33–36
    definition, 25, 27–28
    origins, 25, 26
    priorities, 38–40
    regulatory drivers, 37–38
    transparent convergence, 30–31
    triple-play, 29, 31
North American Electricity
    Reliability Council
    (NERC), 5, 126–128
Nuclear Regulatory Commission, 4

O

Occupational Safety and Health
    Administration (OSHA),
    140
Open Process Control (OPC),
    117, 118
Open Shortest Path First (OSPF),
    35
Open-source tools, 133
Organized crime, 59

OSI protocol, 25
Overall equipment effectiveness, 148–149
Overall equipment effectiveness, security, 149–152

P

Packet injection, 122, 123
Packet storms, 119–120
Passwords, 63
Phishing, 59
Pneumatic systems, 22–23
Porn dialers, 69, 78–79
Process control network (PCN), 50
Process Control System Forum, 3
Process control systems (PCS), 6, 18, 19
    overview, 7
Profibus, 4, 41, 117
Programmable logic controllers (PLCs), 20–21, 107, 110, 116, 118
Protocol inertia, 116–118
Public Safety Canada, 58
Public switched telephone network (PSTN), 29, 101
Purdue Enterprise Reference Architecture (PERA)
    development, 92–93
    level 0, 91
    level 1, 91, 93
    level 2, 90–91
    level 3, 90
    overview, 89

R

Radio-frequency identifier (RFID) tags, 32, 163, 183
Remote access procedures, 101
Remote terminal units (RTUs), 20, 60, 107, 110, 116, 118

Risk assessment; *See also* Security analysis, ICS
    consequence matrices, 138–139
    Control Systems Security Program (CSSP); *See* Control Systems Security Program (CSSP)
    DOE methodology, 136–137
    Homeland Security process, 129–130
    ideal-based metrics, 134, 135
    metrics-based reporting, 133–134
    overall equipment effectiveness, 148–149
    security assurance level; *See* Security assurance level
    security OEE, 149–152
Router announcements (RAs), 169

S

Safety instrumented systems (SIS), 141
    controls, 14
    description of, 14
    design of, 14
    failure rates, 14
    industrial control system (ICS) security, support for, 15
    industrial control system (ICS), *versus*, 8
    IP networks, integration on, 15, 42
    probabilistic threats to, 14–15
    safety requirements, 14
Safety integrity level (SIL), 43, 140
Secure socket layer (SSL), 93
Security analysis, ICS; *See also* Risk assessment
    Control Systems Security Program (CSSP); *See* Control Systems Security Program (CSSP)

Homeland Security ICS risk
assessment process,
129–130
INL National SCADA Test
Bed Program (NSTB),
130–131, 132
National Institute of Standards
and Technology (NIST)
guidelines, 128–129
network-centric analysis, 153–
154, 155–157, 159–160
North American Electricity
Reliability Council
(NERC) guidelines,
126–128
overview, 125
safety integrity level (SIL); *See*
Safety integrity level (SIL)
security assurance level; *See*
Security assurance level
vulnerability assessment
methods, 131–133
Security assurance level, 140
achieved SAL, 143
assessments based on, 144–145
capability SAL, 143
definition, 141
description, 142–143
design SAL, 143
future of, 147–148
SIS, versus, 141–142
target SAL, 143
workflow, 145, 147
Security, industrial control system
(ICS)
acceptance testing, 104–105
accountability, 99–100
administrative roles, 101
age of, 54
analysis of; *See* Security analysis,
ICS
attack vectors, 113–114
best practices, 42

budgeting, 100
business controls, 95
challenges, 1
collateral damage to, 54, 59
consequences of failures of, 8
corporate assets, 62–63
CPU utilization management,
119
cyber threats to, 8
data segregation, 100–101
design of, 53–54
direct strikes, 68
Domain Name Server (DNS)
attacks, 157–159
engagement, management, 100
governance, 99
hardening guidelines, 101–102
importance of, 18
incident detection, 102–103
IT security, *versus*, 8, 9, 50, 53,
99–100
management of, 8, 103–104
manifestations of security
issues, 8
operational controls, 95–96
oversight, 99
overview, 1–2
passwords; *See* Passwords
policies, 99–100
protocol inertia, 116–118
random hits to, 59
remote access procedures, 101
reporting procedures, 102–103
risk assessment; *See* Risk
assessment
seriousness of threats, 28
servers, 102
standards, 1–2, 5–6
technical controls, 96
threats, 54–56
threats-from, 57–58
threats-to, 57, 58, 79–80; *See also*
specific threat types

wireless systems deployment, 101–102
Security, physical, 30
Siemens H1, 24, 117
Six Sigma, 149
Smart phones, 163
SMTP spam engines, 78
Social engineering, 63
Socks proxies, 75, 76–78
Spam, 59, 62, 78
Spam and Open Relay Blocking System (SORBS), 77
SpamHaus, 77
Spoofing, IP, 133
Statement of sensitivity (SOS), 138
Stuxnet, 1, 3
Supervisory control and data acquisition (SCADA), 4, 6, 18, 19
  changes of state, 19
  overview, 19
Symantec, 17, 57

T

Telecommunications regulation, 37
Telepresence, 32
Test Bed Program; *See* National SCADA Test Bed Program (NSTB)
Transmission Control Protocol (TCP), 24, 87, 116
  routing layer, 25
  SYN flood attacks, 145
Transparent convergence, 30–31
Triple play, 27, 29, 31

Trojan horses, 61
Twitter, 63

U

UK Centre for Protection and National Infrastructure, 42
User Datagram Protocol, 86, 87, 156

V

Video streams, encryption of, 88
Virtual LANs (VLANs), 50, 169
Viruses, e-mail, 60
Voice-over IP (VOIP), 29, 37, 84, 87, 93
  presence applications, 34

W

Wide area networks (WANs), 26
WiFi, protocols, 27
WiMax, 102
Windows Media player, 63
World Wide Web, 26
Worms, 60

X

XML, 34

Z

Zero-day exploits, 59, 61
Zombie botnets, 156; *See also* Botnets

*For Product Safety Concerns and Information please contact
our EU representative GPSR@taylorandfrancis.com Taylor & Francis
Verlag GmbH, Kaufingerstraße 24, 80331 München, Germany*

T - #0015 - 230425 - C0 - 234/156/11 [13] - CB - 9781439801963 - Gloss Lamination